Critical
Financial Accounting
Problems

Critical
Financial Accounting
Problems

ISSUES AND SOLUTIONS

Ahmed Riahi-Belkaoui

QUORUM BOOKS
Westport, Connecticut • London

657
R48c

Library of Congress Cataloging-in-Publication Data

Riahi-Belkaoui, Ahmed, 1943–
    Critical financial accounting problems : issues and solutions /
Ahmed Riahi-Belkaoui.
      p. cm.
    Includes bibliographical references and index.
    ISBN 1–56720–116–4 (alk. paper)
    1. Accounting—Standards—United States. 2. Financial Accounting
Standards Board. I. Title.
HF5616.U5R5   1998
657—dc21   97–22748

British Library Cataloguing in Publication Data is available.

Library of Congress Catalog Card Number: 97–22748
ISBN: 1–56720–116–4

First published in 1998

Quorum Books, 88 Post Road West, Westport, CT 06881
An imprint of Greenwood Publishing Group, Inc.

Printed in the United States of America

The paper used in this book complies with the
Permanent Paper Standard issued by the National
Information Standards Organization (Z39.48–1984).

10 9 8 7 6 5 4 3 2 1

To My Family Here and Everywhere.

Contents

Exhibits

Preface

The complexity of the business world and the comprehensive transactions required have led to a proliferation of new accounting standards. This book identifies the main accounting issues that are characterized by their complexity and presents the accounting solutions needed in reporting and disclosure. The coverage of the issues and techniques relies as much on the literature as on the pronouncements of the official U.S. standard-setting bodies, namely, the Financial Accounting Standards Board (FASB). The issues and solutions are covered in eight chapters that include long-term liabilities (Chapter 1), stockholders' equity (Chapter 2), investments (Chapter 3), income taxes (Chapter 4), pensions (Chapter 5), leases (Chapter 6), segmental reporting (Chapter 7), and foreign currency transactions and futures contracts (Chapter 8).

The book should be of interest to financial accounting practitioners, chief financial officers and other executives, as well as for undergraduate and graduate students preparing for any of the numerous professional accounting and finance examinations.

Many people have helped in the development of this book. I received considerable assistance from the University of Illinois at Chicago research assistants, especially Belia Ortega and Dimitra Alvertos. I also thank Eric Valentine, John Donohue, and the entire production team at Quorum Books for their continuous and intelligent support. Finally, to Janice and Hedi, thanks for making everything possible and enjoyable.

1

Long-Term Liabilities

INTRODUCTION

Firms issue long-term bonds and long-term notes as part of their financing strategies. This chapter covers the main issues associated with accounting and reporting of long-term liabilities. The focus is on the Generally Accepted Accounting Principles (GAAP) governing accounting for long-term liabilities.

ACCOUNTING FOR THE ISSUANCE OF BONDS

Bonds Payable

A bond payable is a long-term debt governed by a contract known as *bond indenture* whereby the firm promises to pay the holder (a) the face value at the maturity date and (b) periodic interest on the face value. Common characteristics of a bond include:

a. a face value, par value, principal amount or maturity value

b. a stated, coupon, nominal or contract rate

However, given the general market condition, a *yield (or effective rate)* may prevail in the determination of the bond prices. Three situations may result:

1. The yield is equal to the contract rate and the bonds are sold at par. In such a case the interest expense is equal to the interest paid.

2. The yield is higher than the contract rate and the bonds are sold at a *discount* (the price of the bond is lower than the face value). In such a case, the interest expense is higher than the interest paid.

3. The yield is lower than the contract rate and the bonds are sold at a *premium* (the price of the bond is higher than the face value). In such a case, the interest expense is lower than the interest paid.

To illustrate the potential difference between the bond price and face value, let's assume that the Katori Company issues $200,000 in bonds, due in five years at a contract rate of 9% per year payable at the end of the year. The market rate for the bonds at the time of issuance was 11%. The bond price is the present value of the principal of $200,000 plus the present value of the five year-end annual payments of $18,000. In other words, the selling price or present value of the bonds is as follows:

1. Present value of the principal
   $200,000 × .59345= $118,690.00
2. Present value of the interest payments
   $18,000 × 3.6959= $66,526.20
                                                $185,216.20

Given that the face value of the bond is $200,000, the bonds are selling at a discount of $14,783.80 ($200,000 − $185,216.20), or more explicitly, they were sold for 92.6 (185,216.20/200,000) or 92.6 of par. If the bond price was $220,000, then there would be a premium of $20,000 and the bonds were sold for 110 or 110 of par. The accounting for the three cases of selling at par, selling at a discount and selling at a premium is illustrated next.

Issuance of Bonds at Par on Interest Rate Date

If the bonds are issued at par on interest rate date, only the cash received and the face value of the bonds are recorded. If we assume that on January 1, 1996, the Katori Company had issued $200,000 in bonds, due in five years at a contract rate of 9% per year payable semi-annually, and the market rate was also 9%, then the following entries will be made:

1. On January 1, 1996, to record the issuance

Cash	$200,000	
Bonds Payable		$200,000

2. On July 1, 1996, to record the first semi-annual interest payment of $9,000 (200,000 × 9% × ½)

Bond Interest Expense	$9,000	
Cash		$9,000

3. On December 31, 1996, to record the second semi-annual interest payment of $9,000

Bond Interest Expense	$9,000	
Cash		$9,000

Issuance of Bonds at Discount or Premium on Interest Rate Date

If we assume that on January 1, 1996, the Katori Company had issued $200,000 in bonds, due in five years at a contract rate of 9% and a market rate of 11% then the bonds are sold at a discount of $14,783.80 (as computed earlier), and the following entry is made:

Cash	$185,216.20	
Discount on Bonds Payable	$14,783.80	
Bonds Payable		$200,000

If instead the bonds were sold for $220,000 at a premium of $20,000, then the following entry is made on January 1, 1996:

Cash	$220,000	
Bonds Payable		$200,000
Premium on Bonds Payable		$20,000

In both cases of selling at a discount or premium, the discount on bonds payable or the premium on bonds payable should be amortized using the *straight-line method* or the *effective interest method*.

If the straight-line method is used the entries would have been:

A. In the case of the bonds selling at a discount of $14,783.80, the annual amortization would be $2,956.76 ($14,783.80/5) and the entry at the end of 1996 as follows:

Bond Interest Expense	$2,956.76	
Discount on Bonds Payable		$2,956.76

B. In the case of bonds selling at a premium of $20,000, the annual amortization would be $4,000 ($20,000/5), and the entry at the end of 1996 as follows:

Premium on Bonds Payable	$4,000	
Bond Interest Expense		$4,000

The effective interest method will be illustrated later in the chapter.

Issuance of Bonds between Interest Payment Dates at Par

Bonds are usually issued at their authorization date. They are sometimes sold after their authorization date and between interest payment dates. Because bonds interest payments are made semi-annually, if the bonds are issued between interest payment dates the problem arises of how to treat the *interest accrued from the last interest payment date to the date of the issue.* An effective solution that reduces record keeping for the first interest payment is to add the interest accrued to the selling of the bonds, making the buyer pay for the interest accrued. On the next semi-annual interest payment date, the buyer receives a full six months' interest payment.

To illustrate, assume that on March 1, 1996, the XYZ Corporation issues $160,000 of 10-year bonds dated January 1, 1996, at par and bearing interest at an annual rate of 12% payable semi-annually on January 1 and July 1. The journal entry on March 1, 1996, to record the bond issuance is as follows:

Cash	$163,200	
Bonds Payable		$160,000
Interest Expense (160,000		
$\times$ .12 $\times$ 2/12)		$3,200
(Interest Payable may be credited instead)		

On July 1, 1996, the following entry is made:

Interest Expense		
(160,000 $\times$ .12 $\times$ 6/12)	$9,600	
Cash		$9,600

or

Interest Expense		
(160,000 × .12 × 4/12)	$6,400	
Interest Payable	$3,200	
Cash		$9,600

Effective Interest Method and Bonds Issued at a Discount

The issuance of bonds at a discount raises the need for the amortization of the bond discount. The *effective interest method*, also called the *present value amortization*, will be used. To illustrate, assume that the Teta Company issued, on the first of January 1996, $200,000 of five-year bonds paying semi-annual interest with a stated rate of 12% and an effective interest rate of 14%. The discount may be computed as follows:

1. Present value of principal: 200,000 × .508349 = $101,669.80
2. Present value of interest: 12,000 × 7.023582 = $84,282.98
3. Selling Price $185,952.78
4. Face Value $200,000.00
5. Discount (Face Value − Selling Price) $14,047.22

The journal entry to record the issuance of the bonds follows:

Cash	$185,952.78	
Discount on Bonds Payable	$14,047.22	
Bonds Payable		$200,000.00

The amortization of discount on bonds payable using the effective interest method or present value amortization is computed at every interest payment date as follows:

Amortization Amount = Bond Interest Expense − Bond Interest Paid

where:

Bond Interest Expense = Carrying value of bonds at the beginning of the period × Effective Interest Rate

Exhibit 1.1

Teta Company: Schedule of Bond Discount Amortization, Effective Interest Method, Semi-Annual Interest Payments, 12% Bonds Sold to Yield 14%

Date	Cash Paid (a)	Interest Expense (b)	Discount Amortized (c)	Book Value of Bonds (d)
01/01/96				$185,952.78
06/30/96	$12,000	$13,016.69	$1,016.69	$186,969.47
12/31/96	$12,000	$13,087.86	$1,087.86	$188,057.33
06/30/97	$12,000	$13,164.01	$1,164.01	$189,057.33
12/31/97	$12,000	$13,245.49	$1,254.49	$190,466.83
06/30/98	$12,000	$13,332.67	$1,332.67	$191,799.50
12/31/98	$12,000	$13,425.96	$1,425.96	$193,225.46
06/30/99	$12,000	$13,525.78	$1,525.78	$194,751.24
12/31/99	$12,000	$13,632.58	$1,632.58	$196,383.82
06/30/00	$12,000	$13,746.86	$1,746.86	$198,130.68
12/31/00	$12,000	$13,869.14	$1,869.14	$200,000.00

(a) $200,000 (face value) $\times$ 0.12 (stated rate) $\times$ ½ year
(b) Previous book value $\times$ 0.14 (effective rate) $\times$ ½ year
(c) (b) − (a)
(d) Previous book value + (c)

> Carrying Value   = Face Value minus any unamortized discount plus any unamortized premium
>
> Bond Interest Paid   = Face Amount of Bonds $\times$ Stated Interest Rate

The computation of the bond interest expense and discount amortization schedule is shown in Exhibit 1.1. It is used on June 30, 1996, to make the following entry:

Bond Interest Expense	$13,016.69	
Discount on Bonds Payable		$1,016.69
Cash		$12,000.00

The following entry is made on December 31, 1996:

Bond Interest Expense	$13,087.86

Discount on Bonds Payable	$1,087.86	
Cash		$12,000.00

Effective Interest Method and Bonds Issued at a Premium

To illustrate, assume that on January 1, 1996, the Smith Company issued $200,000 of five-year bonds paying semi-annual interest with a stated rate of 12% and an effective interest rate of 10%. The premium may be computed as follows:

1. Present Value of principal: $200,000 × 0.613913 =	$122,782.60
2. Present Value of interest: $12,000 × 7.721735 =	$92,660.82
3. Selling Price	$215,443.42
4. Face Value	$200,000.00
5. Premium	$15,443.42

The journal entry to record the issuance of the bonds follows:

Cash	$215,443.42	
Premium on Bonds Payable		$15,442.42
Bonds Payable		$200,000.00

The computation of the bond interest expense and premium amortization schedule is shown in Exhibit 1.2. It is used on June 30, 1996, to make the following entry:

Bond Interest Expense	$10,772.17	
Premium on Bonds Payable	$1,227.83	
Cash		$12,000.00

Accruing Bond Interest

When interest payment dates and the date of the financial statements issuance are not the same, there is a need for accounting for accrual of interest and a partial premium or discount amortization to be made at the end of the fiscal year. For example, let's assume that the previous example of the Smith Company includes a need to report the financial statements by the end of March 1996. In that case the matching concept

Exhibit 1.2
Smith Company: Schedule of Bond Premium Amortization, Effective Interest Method, Semi-Annual Interest Payments, 12% Bonds Sold to Yield 10%

Date	Cash Paid (a)	Interest Expense (b)	Premium Amortized (c)	Book Value of Bonds (d)
01/01/96				$215,443.42
06/30/96	$12,000	$10,772.17	$1,227.83	$214,215.59
12/31/96	$12,000	$10,710.77	$1,289.22	$212,926.37
06/30/97	$12,000	$10,646.31	$1,353.68	$211,572.69
12/31/97	$12,000	$10,578.63	$1,421.36	$210,151.33
06/30/98	$12,000	$10,507.56	$1,492.43	$208,658.90
12/31/98	$12,000	$10,432.94	$1,567.05	$207,091.85
06/30/99	$12,000	$10,354.59	$1,645.40	$205,466.45
12/31/99	$12,000	$10,272.32	$1,727.67	$203,718.78
06/30/00	$12,000	$10,185.93	$1,814.06	$201,904.72
12/31/00	$12,000	$10,095.23	$1,904.76	$200,000.00

(a) $200,000 (face value) $\times$ 0.12 (stated rate) $\times$ ½ year
(b) Previous book value $\times$ 0.14 (effective rate) $\times$ ½ year
(c) (a) − (b)
(d) Previous book value − (c)

dictates a proration over three months of interest and premium amortized as follow:

1. Premium amortized (1,227.83 $\times$ 3/6) $613.915
2. Interest Expense (10,772.17 $\times$ 3/6) $5,386.085
3. Interest Payable (12,000 $\times$ 3/6) $6,000.000

The journal entry at the end of March 1996 to record the accrual is as follows:

Interest Expense	$5,386.085	
Premium on Bonds Payable	$613.915	
Interest Payable		$6,000.000

Costs of Issuing Bonds

Various expenditures may be required for the issuance of bonds, including legal and accounting fees, printing costs and registration fees. The present GAAP requirement is to defer the costs of issuing bonds and amortize over the life of the bond issue by the straight-line method. To illustrate, assume that on January 1, 1996, Tucker Company issued five-year bonds with a face value of $10,000,000 and a price of $10,500,000. Expenditures connected with the issue amounted to $250,000. The journal entry to record the issue is as follows:

Cash (10,500,000 − 250,000)	$10,250,000	
Unamortized Bond Issue Costs	$250,000	
Premium on Bonds Payable		$500,000
Bonds Payable		$10,000,000

The journal entry on December 31, 1996, to record the amortization is as follows:

Bond Interest Expense	$50,000	
Unamortized Bond Issue Costs		$50,000
(250,000/5)		

The unamortized bond issue costs are to be disclosed as deferred charge on other assets.

Bonds Issued with Detachable Warrants

Bonds issued with detachable warrants allow the bondholder to acquire a specific number of common shares at a given price and a given time. The bonds are known as bonds with stock warrants or stock rights. The proceeds of the bonds are allocated to both the bonds and the warrants as follows:

1. Amount Allocated to Bonds $= \dfrac{\text{Market Value of Bonds without Warrants}}{\text{Market Value of Bonds without Warrants} + \text{Market Value of Warrants}} \times \text{Issuance Price}$

2. Amount
   Allocated $=$
   to Warrant

$$\frac{\text{Market Value of Warrant}}{\text{Market Value of Bonds Without Warrants} + \text{Market Value of Warrants}} \times \begin{array}{c}\text{Issuance} \\ \text{Price}\end{array}$$

To illustrate, let's assume that the Dimitra Company sold $400,000 of 12% bonds at 101 or $404,000. Each $1,000 bond is issued with 10 detachable warrants that entitle the holder to acquire one share of $10 par common stock for $30 per share. Following the issuance the bonds without the rights attached (ex. rights) were quoted at 99 and the warrants at $3 each. The proceeds of the bonds are allocated as follows:

1. Amount
   Allocated $= \dfrac{\$990 \times 400}{(990 \times 400) + (3 \times 400 \times 10)} \times \$404{,}000 = \$392{,}117.68$
   to Bonds

2. Amount
   Allocated $= \dfrac{\$3 \times 400 \times 10}{(990 \times 400) + (3 \times 400 \times 10)} \times \$404{,}000 = \$11{,}882.396$
   to Warrant

As a result the following entry may be made:

Cash	$404,000.00	
Discount on Bonds Payable		
(400000 − 392117.68)	$7,882.32	
Bonds Payable		$400,000.00
Common Stock Warrants		11,882.32

The value of each warrant is $2.96 (11882.32/4000). Assuming 100 warrants were exercised, the following entry will be made:

Cash ($30 × 100)	$3,000.00	
Common Stock Warranty		
(2.97 × 100)	$297.00	
Common Stock (10 × 100)		$1,000.00
Additional Paid-in Capital		
on Common Stock		$2,297.00

If all the remaining warrants expire, the following entry is made:

Common Stock Warrants	$11,585.32	
Additional Paid-in Capital		
on Common Stock		$11,585.32

Accounting for Convertible Bonds and Preferred Stock

Convertible bonds are bonds that can be converted into common stocks, allowing the bondholder (a creditor) to become a stockholder by exchanging the bonds for a specified number of shares. Issuance of convertible bonds may be motivated by making an increase in equity later or an increase in bonds now, more attractive through the conversion feature. Other factors that may motivate a firm to issue convertible bonds is related to its desire to:

1. Avoid the downward price pressure on its stock that placing a large new issue of common stock on the market would cause
2. Avoid the direct sale of common stock when it believes its stock currently is undervalued in the market
3. Penetrate that segment of the capital market that is unwilling or unable to participate in a direct common stock issue
4. Minimize the costs associated with selling securities.[1]

The first accounting problem facing convertible debts is the accounting at the time of issuance. Following APB Opinion No. 14,[2] accounting for convertible debt at the time of issuance treats it solely as a debt, with the discount or premium amortized to its maturity date. The second accounting problem arises at the time of conversion. Two methods may be used for recording the conversion.

1. *Book Value Method.* Under this method the stockholders' equity (common stock and additional paid-in capital) is credited at the book value of convertible bonds on the date of conversion, resulting in no gain or loss being recognized.
2. *Market Value Method.* Under this method the stockholders' equity (common stock and additional paid-in capital) is credited at the market value of the shares issued on the date of conversion, resulting in the recognition of a gain or loss to be included as ordinary rather than extraordinary income.

To illustrate both methods, let's assume that the Bulls Corporation has issued $20,000 worth of convertible bonds that have now a book value of $21,000. Each $1,000 bond is convertible into 20 shares of common stock (par value $40). At the time of conversion, interest had been paid on the debt, and the market value of the common stock is $60 per share. The entries under both methods would be:

A. Under the Book Value Method:

Bonds Payable	$20,000	
Premium on Bonds Payable	$1,000	
Common Stock		
(40 × 20 × 20)		$16,000
Additional Paid-in Capital		
from Bond Conversion		$5,000
(21,000 − 16,000)		

B. Under the Market Value Method:

Bonds Payable	$20,000	
Premium on Bonds Payable	$1,000	
Loss on Conversion		
(48,000 − 21,000)	$27,000	
Common Stock		
(40 × 20 × 20)		$16,000
Additional Paid-in Capital		
from Bond Conversion		$32,000
(40 × 20 × 40)		

Let's assume that in the previous example the firm has agreed to pay an extra $5,000 to the bondholders to induce conversion; the following entry under the book value method will be made:

Debt Conversion Expense	$5,000	
Bonds Payable	$20,000	
Premium on Bonds Payable	$1,000	
Common Stock		$16,000
Additional Paid-in Capital		$5,000
Cash		$5,000

The cash used to induce conversion is treated as an ordinary expense of the current period.

Upon retirement of a convertible debt, the difference between the cash acquisition price of the debt and its carrying amount is treated as an extraordinary gain or loss on extinguishment of debt.[3] The book value is generally preferred because it avoids the type of manipulation of income through gain or loss as permitted under the market value method. However, for convertible preferred stock, *only the book value method is permitted for conversion where*:

a. Convertible preferred stock and additional paid-in capital is debited.

b. Common stock and additional paid-in capital (in case an excess exists) is credited.

c. Retained earning is debited if the par value of the common stock exceeds the par value of preferred stock.

To illustrate, let's assume that the Green Company issued 5,000 shares of common stock (par value $10) upon conversion of 5,000 shares of preferred stock (par value $5) that has been previously used with a premium of $800. The entry is as follows:

Convertible Preferred Stock		
(5,000 × 5)	$25,000	
Paid-in Capital in Excess of Par		
(Premium on Preferred Stock)	$800	
Retained Earnings		
(50,000 − 25,800)	$24,200	
Common Stock		
(5,000 × 10)		$50,000

Some states require, however, that the additional return used to induce conversion should be debited to paid-in capital.

ACCOUNTING FOR EXTINGUISHMENT AND DEFEASANCE

Long-term debt may be retired either through an extinguishment of debt (Reacquisition of Debt) or a defeasance of debt (In-Substance Defeasance of Debt). Both practices are examined next.

Reacquisition of Debt

Bonds may be reacquired at maturity or prior to maturity. If the bonds are reacquired at maturity, the premium or discount and issue costs are fully amortized, and the face value of the bond is equal to the market value at the time resulting in no gain or loss.

If the bonds are retired before maturity or replaced with a new issue (refunding) a different situation arises. First, the *net carrying amount* of the bonds is adjusted for amortized premium, discount and cost of issuance. Second, the difference between the net carrying amount and the *reacquisition price (call price)* is either a gain or loss from extinguishment. All material gains and losses from debt extinguishment (both retirements and refunding) are classified as extraordinary item in the year of cancellation. To illustrate, let's assume that the Mavrides Corporation had issued $200,000 worth of 10-year bonds paying 12% at 97 on January 1, 1995. The bonds, paying interest on January 1 and July 1, and callable at 105 plus accrued interest, were recalled on June 30, 2000. Two entries are required. The first entry is used to record the current interest expense as well as the amortization of the expired discount, is as follows:

Interest Expense	$12,300	
Discount on Bonds Payable		
(6000 / 10) × ½		$300
Interest Payable		
(200,000 × .12 × ½)		$12,000

The second entry, used to record the reacquisition of debt, is as follows:

Bonds Payable	$200,000	
Interest Payable	$12,000	
Extraordinary loss on		
Bond Redemption	$12,700	
Discount on Bonds Payable		$2,700
Cash		$222,000

where:

a. the discount on bonds payable is computed as
   1. The original discount $6,000
   2. Amortized on a straight-line
      basis for 5½ years:
      5.5 × 600   ($3,300)

3. Unamortized discount $2,700

b. Cash = $200,000 × 1.05 + 12,000

c. Extraordinary loss on bond redemption:
    1. Call price (excluding interest) $210,000
    2. Less: Face Value $200,000
         unamortized discount   ($2,700)   ($197,300)
                                                     $12,700

In-Substance Defeasance

In-substance defeasance of debt is an arrangement whereby the debtor places cash or purchased securities in an irrevocable trust to be used solely to pay off the interest and principal of debt. To illustrate in-substance defeasance of debt, let's assume that on January 1, 1996, The Das Company issued $100,000 of five-year, 12% bonds that yield 10%. On December 31, 1998, when the book value of the bonds is $103,545.92, The Das Company purchased $96,545.92 in $100,000, 12% U.S. government bonds to service the bond interest and principal and extinguish its debt. The journal entry to record this extinguishment is as follows:

Bonds Payable	$100,000.00	
Premium on Bonds Payable	$ 3,545.92	
Cash		$96,545.92
Extraordinary Gain on		
Bond Extinguishment		$7,000.00

LONG-TERM NOTES PAYABLE

Long-term notes differ form short-term notes on the basis of different maturities. They differ from long-term bonds on the term of tradability on organized public securities markets. Like a bond, a note payable is recorded at the present value of its future interest and principal cash flows, with any discount or premium amortized over the life of the note. Similarly, interest expense is recorded over the life of the note on the basis of the effective interest method. Examples of issuance of long-term notes payable follow:

Issuance of a Note at Face Value

Let's return to the section on Bonds Payable and assume the same facts for the Katori Company except that the firm issued a long-term note rather than bonds. Because the stated rate and the effective rate are the same, the present value of the note and its face value at the time of issuance are the same, resulting in no premium or discount. Accordingly, the entry at the time of issuance is as follows:

Cash	$200,000	
Notes Payable		$200,000

On July 1, 1996, to record the first semi-annual interest payment of $9,000 (200000 × 9% × ½):

Interest Expense	$9,000	
Cash		$9,000

Issuance of a Note at Other than Face Value and Zero Interest

Notes issued at other than face value and at zero interest are known as zero coupon bonds. The difference between the face value and the cash received (present value) is either a discount or premium to be amortized to interest expense over the life of the note. To illustrate, let's assume that the Ignacius Corporation issued three-year, $20,000, zero coupon bonds for $15,443.60, that is, with a discount of $4,556.40. The present value of the note is $15,443.60. Therefore 15,443.60 equals present value of three-year at interest rate (i) of $20,000.

$$\text{Present value at interest rate (i) for 3 years} = \frac{\$15,443.60}{\$20,0000.00} = 0.77218$$

The present value table shows that 0.77218 is the present value of a $1 for three periods at 9%. Therefore, the implicit interest rate is 9%. Exhibit 1.3 shows the amortization of the note discount using the effective interest method. The two main entries follow:

1. At the time of issuance
   Cash $15,443.60

Exhibit 1.3
Schedule of Note Discount Amortization, Effective Interest Method, 10%
Note Discounted at 9%

	Cash Paid	Interest Expense	Discount Amortized	Carrying Amount of Note
Date of Issue				$15,433.60
End of Year 1	$ ---0---	$1,389.924 (a)	$1,389.924 (b)	$16,833.524 (c)
End of Year 2	$ ---0---	$1,515.017	$1,515.017	$18,348.541
End of Year 3	$ ---0---	$1,651.458	$1,651.458	$20,000.00 (d)

(a) = $15,443.60 × .09 = $1,389.924
(b) = (a) − 0
(c) = $15,443.60 + $1,389.924
(d) = rounded

Discount on Notes Payable	$4,556.40
Notes Payable	$20,000.00

2. At the end of the first year

Interest Expense	$1,389.924	
Discount on Notes Payable		$1,389.924

Issuance of a Note at Other than Face Value and with Interest

Let's assume that the Ignacius Corporation issues now a $20,000, three-year note bearing a stated interest of 10%. The market rate for a similar note is 12%.

The present value of the note is equal to:
a. the present value of the principal = $20,000(0.7118) = $14,326.00
b. the present value of the interest = $2,000(2.40183) = $ 4,803.66
c. the present value of the note $19,039.66

  The face value of the note is equal to $20,000

  The discount is equal to ($20,000 − $19,039.66) = $ 960.34

Therefore, at the time of issuance, the following entry is made:

  Cash $19,039.66

Exhibit 1.4
Schedule of Note Discount Amortization, 10% Note Discounted at 12%

	Cash Paid	Interest Expense	Discount Amortized	Carrying Amount of Note
Date of Issue				$19,039.66
End of Year 1	$2,000 (a)	$2,284.759 (b)	$284.759 (c)	$19,324.419 (d)
End of Year 2	$2,000	$2,318.930	$318.930	$19,643.349
End of Year 3	$2,000	$2,357.201	$357.201	$20,000.00

(a) = $20,000 × 0.10 = $2,000
(b) = $19,039.66 × 0.12 = $2,284.759
(c) = (b) − (a)
(d) = $19,039.66 + (c)

Discount on Notes Payable	$960.34
Notes Payable	$20,000

Exhibit 1.4 shows the amortization of the note discount using the effective interest method. The entry at the end of the year is as follows:

Interest Expense	$2,284.759
Discount on Bonds Payable	$284.759
Cash	$2,000.000

Issuance of Notes in Exchange for Cash and Rights or Privileges

Notes may be issued for cash and include special rights or privileges. One example of rights or privileges is the right for the holders of the note to buy certain goods from the company at lower than the prevailing prices. The difference between the present value of the note and the amount of cash received is recorded as a discount on the note to be debited and an unearned revenue to be credited. The discount is to be amortized as a charge to interest expense using the effective interest method. The unearned revenue is amortized as revenue over the life of the contract on the basis of appropriate revenue recognition criteria; for example, in the same proportion as the period sales to total sales to the customers.

Let's assume that the Clinton Company borrowed $200,000 by issuing a three-year, non-interest-bearing note to a customer that allows the customer to buy equal amount of goods from the Clinton Company at reduced prices over a 10-year period. The company's incremental borrowing rate is 12%. Therefore the present value of the note is $142,356 (200000 × 0.71180).

Following are the entries made:

A. At the time of issuance

Cash		$200,000
Discount on Notes Payable	$57,644	
(200,000 – 142,356)		
Notes Payable	$200,000	
Unearned Revenue	$57,644	

B. At the end of the first year

Interest Expense (142,356 × .12)	$17,082.72	
Discount on Notes Payable		$17,082.72
Unearned Revenue (57,644 / 10)	$5,764.40	
Sales Revenue		$5,764.40

C. End of the second year

Interest Expense [(142,356 + 17,082.72) × .12]	$19,132.646	
Discount on Notes Payable		$19,132.646
Unearned Revenue	$ 5,764.40	
Sales Revenue		$5,764.40

Issuance of Notes in Exchange for Property, Goods or Services

Notes may be issued in exchange for property, goods or services. The stated interest rate is presumed fair unless:

1. No interest rate is stated, or
2. The stated interest rate is unreasonable, or
3. The face value of the note is materially different from the current cash sales price of the property, goods or service, or from the current market value of the note.

In this case, the fair market value of the note is used as the present value of the note. When there is no stated interest rate, the interest element is the difference between the face value of the note and the fair value of the property.

To illustrate, let's assume that on January 1, 1996, the Weygandt Company purchased equipment with a useful life of five years from the Zribi Company, for a non-interest-bearing, $30,000 five-year note. The Weygandt Company's incremental borrowing rate is 12%. Therefore, the present value of $30,000 to be repaid at the end of five years at 12% is $17,022.81 (30000 × 0.567427). The following entries are made:

1. At the date of issuance

Equipment	$17,022.81	
Discount on Notes Payable	$12,977.19	
Notes Payable		$30,000.00

2. At the end of the first year

Interest Expense		
[(30,000 − 12,977.19) × .12]	$2,042.73	
Discount on Notes Payable		$2,042.73
Depreciation Expense	$3,404.56	
Accumulated Depreciation		$3,404.56

3. At the end of the second year

Interest Expense	$1797.60	
[(30,000 − (12,977.19 +		
2,042.73)) × .12]		
Discount on Notes Payable		$1797.60
Depreciation Expense	$3,404.56	
Accumulated Depreciation		$3,404.56

Issuance of Notes with Imputed Interest

If the stated rate is found to be unreasonable, an imputed interest rate is required, leading to a discount or a premium to be amortized. For example, let's assume that on December 31, 1996, the Pegg Company issued a note to the Alvertos Company, for the purchase of a building, with a face value of $600,000, a due date of December 1, 2000 and a stated interest rate of 2%. The market conditions dictated than an 8% interest rate should be imputed for the case.

Exhibit 1.5
Schedule of Note Discount Amortization with Imputed Interest

Date	Cash Paid (2%)	Interest Expense (8%)	Discount Amortized	Carrying Amount of Note
12/31/96				$456,260.52
12/31/97	$12,000 (a)	$36,500.841 (b)	$24,500.841 (c)	$480,761.36
12/31/98	$12,000	$38,460.908	$26,460.908	$507,222.26
12/31/99	$12,000	$40,577.78	$28,577.78	$535,800.04
12/31/00	$12,000	$42,864.003	$30,864.003	$566,664.04
12/31/01	$12,000	$45,333.123	$33,333.123	$600,000.00

(a) = $600,000 × 2% = $12,000
(b) = $456,260.52 × 8% = $36,500.841
(c) = $36,500.841 − $12,000 = $24,500.841

A. The present value of the note is equal to:
    1. Present value of $600,000 due in 5 years
       at 6% per year = 600,000 × .68058 = $408,348.00
    2. Present value of $12,000 interest payable
       per year for 5 years at 8% = 12,000 ×
       3.99271 = $47,912.52
    3. Present value of the note = $456,260.52
B. The face value of the note is equal to $600,000.00
C. The discount of the note is equal to (600,000 − $143,739.48
    456,260.52)

Therefore the entry at the date of issuance is as follows:

Building	$456,260.52	
Discount on Notes Payable	$143,739.48	
Notes Payable		$600,000.00

Exhibit 1.5 shows the schedule of note discount amortization using the effective interest method. At the end of the first year, the entry for the first year's interest and discount amortization is as follows:

Interest Expense	$36,508.84

| Discount on Notes Payable | $24,500.84 |
| Cash | $12,000.00 |

ACCOUNTING FOR LOAN IMPAIRMENTS

Loan impairment arises when it is probable that the creditor may not be able to collect all of the principal and interest due on a loan. For example, let's assume that on December 31, 1996, the Gore Company issued a $1,000,000, five-year, non-interest-bearing note to the First Security Bank, yielding 10% per year. At the date of the issuance the Gore Company paid $620,920 (1,000,000 × 0.62092). The following entries were made:

A. By the creditor, the First Security Bank

Notes Receivable	$1,000,000	
Discount on Notes		
Receivable		$379,080
Cash		$620,920

B. By the debtor, the Gore Company

Cash	$620,920	
Discount on Notes Payable		$379,080
Notes Payable		$1,000,000

Exhibit 1.6 shows the note discount amortization using the effective interest method. Now, let's assume that because of bad economic conditions for the Gore Company, the First Security Bank estimates on December 31, 1998, that only $800,000 is collectable at the end of the five years. Therefore, it estimates its loss due to impairment as follows:

1. Carrying amount of the loan, 12/31/98	$751,312.20
2. Present value of $800,000 due in 3 years at 10% compounded annually (800,000 × 0.75132)	$601,056.00
3. Loss due to impairment (751,312.20 − 601,056)	$150,256.20

Therefore, the First Security Bank made the following entry:

Bad Debt Expense	$150,256.20	
Allowance for Doubtful		
Accounts		$150,256.20

Exhibit 1.6
First Security Bank: First Loan Amortization Schedule

Date	Cash Received	Interest Revenue (10%)	Discount Amortized	Carrying Amount of Note
12/31/96				$620,920.00
12/31/97	$ ---0---	$62,092.00 (a)	$62,092.00	$683,012.00 (b)
12/31/98	$ ---0---	$68,301.20	$68,301.20	$751,313.20
12/31/99	$ ---0---	$75,131.32	$75,131.32	$856,444.52
12/31/00	$ ---0---	$82,644.452	$82,644.452	$909,088.97
12/31/01	$ ---0---	$90,908.897	$90,908.897	$1,000,000.00

(a) = $620,920 × 0.10 = $62,092
(b) = $620.920 + $62,092 = $683,012.00

The Gore Company does not make an entry. The First Security Bank prepares a new schedule of discount amortization based on the new carrying amount of $601,056. It is shown in Exhibit 1.7. The following entries are made on Dec. 31, 1999:

A. By the First Security Bank

Discount on Notes Receivable	$75,131.32	
Interest Revenue		$60,105.60
Allowance for Doubtful		
Accounts		$15,025.72

B. By the Gore Company

Interest Expense	$75,131.32	
Discount on Notes Payable		$75,131.32

At the maturity date, on January 1, 2000, the Gore Company pays $800,000 and the following entries are made:

A. By the First Security Bank

Cash	$800,000	
Allowance for Doubtful		
Accounts	$200,000	
Notes Receivable		$1,000,000

Exhibit 1.7
First Security Bank: Second Loan Amortization Schedule

Date	Cash Received	Interest Revenue (10%)	Discount Amortized	Carrying Amount of Note
12/31/98				$601,056.00
12/31/99	$ ---0---	$60,105.60 (a)	$60,105.60	$661,161.60 (b)
12/31/00	$ ---0---	$66,116.16	$66,116.16	$727,277.76
12/31/01	$ ---0---	$72,727.776	$72,727.776	$800,000.00

(a) = $601,056.00 × 10% = $60,105.60
(b) = $601,056.00 + $60,105.60 = $661,161.60

B. By the Gore Company

Notes Payable	$1,000,000	
Cash		$800,000
Gain on Extinguishment		$200,000

Accounting for Troubled Debt Restructuring

As stated in FASB Statement No. 15, a troubled debt restructuring crisis occurs when a creditor "for economic or legal reasons related to the debtor's financial difficulties grants a concession to the debtor that it would not otherwise consider." The troubled debt restructuring may take one of two forms:

1. Settlement of debt at less than its carrying amount
2. Modification of terms of the debt.

Settlement of Debt

A debt may be settled by an equity or asset exchange. In either case, the equity or the asset should be valued at its fair market value.

For example, let's assume that on December 31, 1996, the Kurk Company exchanges 40,000 of its own shares to a bank holding a note payable and accrued interest totaling $1,800,000. The accrued interest amounts to $800,000. The shares have a par value of $10 per share and a market price of $30 per share. At the date of equity exchange the following entry is initiated by the Kurk Company:

Notes Payable	$1,000,000	
Interest Payable	$800,000	
Common Stock		
(40,000 × 10)		$400,000
Additional Paid-in Capital		
(40,000 × 20)		$800,000
Extraordinary Gain on Debt		
Restructure		$600,000

At the same date, the following entry is made by the bank:

Investment in Kurk	$1,200,000	
Loss on Restructured Loan	$600,000	
Notes Receivable		$1,000,000
Interest Receivable		$800,000

Let's assume now that instead of exchanging equity, the Kurk Company decided to exchange land it bought five years ago for $800,000, and which has a current market value of $1,000,000. In such a case, the Kurk Company initiates the following entry:

Notes Payable	$1,200,000	
Interest Payable	$600,000	
Extraordinary Gain on Debt		
Restructure		$800,000
Gain on Disposal of Land		$200,000
Land		$800,000

At the same date, the following entry is made by the bank:

Land	$1,000,000	
Loss on Restructured Loan	$800,000	
Notes Receivable		$1,000,000
Interest Receivable		$800,000

In both the asset and equity exchange, the bank would have changed the loss (or gain) on a restructured loan to allowance for doubtful accounts if an allowance was available.

Modification of Terms

The debtor may ask for a modification of terms. Some of the possible modifications include:

a. Deduction of the stated interest rate,
b. Extension of the maturity date,
c. Reduction of the face amount of the debt,
d. Reduction of accrued interest.

The accounting for modification of terms differs between the debtor and the creditor. The debtor computes the new loan on the basis of *undiscounted* future cash payments (principal plus interest) specified by the new terms, while the creditor relies on *discounted amounts*. Two situations may arise for the debtor:

Situation 1: When the undiscounted restructured cash flows are higher than (or equal to) the carrying value of the liability, no gain is recognized by the debtor, the carrying value of the liability is not reduced and a new effective rate is used to record the interest expense in future periods.

Situation 2: When the undiscounted restructured cash flows are lower than the carrying value of the liability, a gain is recognized by the debtor, the carrying value of the liability is reduced, and no interest expense is recognized in future periods.

Both situations are examined next.

No Gain Is Recognized by Debtor

To illustrate situation 1 where no gain is recognized by the debtor, let's assume that on December 31, 1996, the Mario Company restructures a $12,671,092 debt with its bank that includes a principal of $12,000,000 and accrued interest of $671,092. The new terms include:

1. Forgiving the $671,092 accrued interest
2. Reducing the principal by $2,000,000
3. Extending the maturity date from December 31, 1996 to December 31, 2000, and
4. Reducing the interest rate from 12% to 10%.

Exhibit 1.8
Mario Company: Schedule of Interest Computation

Date	Cash Paid (10%)	Interest Expense (4%)	Reduction of Carrying Amount	Carrying Value of the Note
12/31/95				$12,671,092
12/31/96	$1,000,000 (a)	$506,843.68 (b)	$493,156.40	$12,177,936 (c)
12/31/97	$1,000,000	$487,117.44	$512,882.60	$11,665,054
12/31/98	$1,000,000	$466,602.16	$533,397.90	$11,131,657
12/31/99	$1,000,000	$445,266.28	$554,733.80	$10,576,924
12/31/00	$1,000,000	$423,076.96	$10,576,924	$ ---0---

(a) = $10,000,000 × .10
(b) = $12,671,092 × .04
(c) = $12,671,092 − $493,156.40

The total future cash payments resulting from the new terms are $15,000,000 (principal of $10,000,000 at the end of five years and interest of $5,000,000 at the end of each year for five years). Because the undiscounted amount of principal and interest of $15,000,000 is higher than the carrying value of the liability of $12,671,052, no gain is recognized and the carrying value of the liability is not reduced. However, the difference of $2,328,908 is recognized as interest expense using the effective interest method. The effective interest rate is obtained by solving for i in the following formula:

$$\$12,671,092 = \frac{1}{(1 + i)^5} \times 1,000,000 + \frac{1 - \dfrac{1}{(1 + i)^5}}{(i)} \times 1,000,000$$

Solving the equation leads to (i) = 4%.

Therefore, on December 31, 1995, the Mario Company makes the following entry to transfer the accrued interest payable balance to the Notes Payable account as follows:

Interest Payable	$671,092	
Notes Payable		$671,092

Exhibit 1.8 shows the computation of the interest expense. Therefore,

on December 31, 1997 (and at the end of each year), the Mario Company makes the following entry:

Notes Payable	$493,156.40	
Interest Expense	$506,842.60	
Cash		$1,000,000

At the end of the year 2000, the following entry will be made:

Notes Payable	$10,576,924	
Interest Expense	$423,076	
Cash		$11,000,000

The situation is different for the bank. It computes the loss on restructuring as follows:

A. Present value of restructured cash flows:
   1. Present value of $10,000,000 due in 5
      years at 12%
      (10,000,000 × 0.56743)   =$5,674,300
   2. Present value of $1,000,000 interest payable
      annually for 5 years at 12% (1,000,000 ×
      3.60478   =$3,604,780
   3. Present value of restructured value   =$9,279,080
B. Pre-Restructure Value   =$12,671,092
C. Loss on Restructuring (12,671,092 − 9,279,080)   =$3,392,012

Accordingly, the bank makes the following entry on 12/31/95:

Allowance for Doubtful		
Accounts	$3,392,012	
Notes Receivable		$3,392,012

Exhibit 1.9 shows the computation of interest revenue. Therefore, on December 31, 1997, the bank makes the following entry:

Cash	$1,000,000.00	
Notes Receivable	$113,489.60	
Interest Revenue		$1,113,489.60

At maturity the following additional entry is made:

Exhibit 1.9
Schedule of Computation of Interest Revenue

Date	Cash Received (a) 10%	Interest Expense (b) 12%	Discount Amortized (c)	Carrying Value of the Note
12/31/95				$9,279,080
12/31/96	$1,000,00	$1,113,489.60	$113,489.60	$9,392,569.60 (d)
12/31/97	$1,000,000	$1,127,108.30	$127,108.30	$9,519,677.90
12/31/98	$1,000,000	$1,142,361.30	$142,361.30	$9,662,039.20
12/31/99	$1,000,000	$1,159,444.70	$159,444.70	$9,821,483.90
12/31/00	$1,000,000	$1,178,578.00	$178,578.00	$10,000,000.00

(a) = $10,000,000 × 10%
(b) = $9,879,080 × 12%
(c) = $1,113,489.60 − $1,000,000
(d) = $9,279,080 + $113,489.60

Cash	$10,000,000	
Notes Receivable		$10,000,000

A Gain Is Recognized by Debtor

To illustrate situation 2, let's assume the same facts as in the previous example, except that the bank reduced the principal by $6,000,000. In such a case, the total future cash payments resulting from the new terms are $9,000,000 (principal of $6,000,000 at the end of five years and interest of $3,000,000 at the end of each year for five years). Because the undiscounted amount of principal and interest of $9,000,000 is less than the carrying value of the liability of $12,671,092, the Mario Company will reduce its liability by $3,671,092 and recognize an extraordinary gain of $3,671,092. However, the bank computes its loss on restructuring as follows:

A. Present value of restructured cash flows:
  1. Present value of $6,000,000 due in 5 years
     at 12% (6,000,000 × 0.56743)   = $3,404,580
  2. Present value of $600,000 interest payable
     annually for 5 years at 12% (600,000 ×
     3.60478)   + $2,162,868
  3. Present value of restructured cash flows   = $5,567,448

Exhibit 1.10
Schedule of Interest Revenue Computations

Date	Interest Received (10%)	Interest Revenue (12%)	Increase in Carrying Amount	Carrying Amount of the Note
12/31/95				$5,567,448.00
12/31/96	$600,000 (a)	$668,093.76 (b)	$68,093.76 (c)	$5,635,541.70
12/31/97	$600,000	$676,265.00	$76,256.00	$5,711,806.70
12/31/98	$600,000	$685,416.80	$85,416.80	$5,797,223.50
12/31/99	$600,000	$695,666.82	$95,666.82	$5,892,890.30
12/31/00	$600,000	$707,146.83	$107,141.83	$6,000,000.00

(a) = $6,000,000 × 0.10
(b) = $5,567,488 × 0.12
(c) = $668,093.76 − $600,000.00

B. Pre-Restructure Value   = $12,671,092
C. Loss on Restructuring (12,671,092 − 5,567,448)   = $7,103,644

The following entries are made on December 31, 1996:

A. By the Mario Company

Notes Payable	$3,671,092	
Gain on Restructuring of Debt		$3,671,092

B. By the Bank

Allowance for Doubtful Accounts	$7,103,644	
Notes Receivable		$6,000,000
Discount on Notes Receivable		$1,103,644

Exhibit 1.10 shows the schedule of interest revenue computation for the bank. The following entries are made:

A. By the Mario Company
December 31, 1997/98/99/00

Notes Payable	$600,000	

Cash		$600,000
December 31, 2000		
Notes Payable	$6,000,000	
Cash		$6,000,000

B. By the Bank

December 31, 1997		
Cash	$600,000.00	
Discount on Notes Receivable	$68,093.76	
Interest Revenue		$668,093.76
December 31, 2000		
Cash	$6,000,000	
Notes Receivable		$6,000,000

CONCLUSIONS

This chapter covered the main techniques associated with accounting for long-term liabilities in conformity with the GAAP.

NOTES

1. Loren A. Nikolai and John D. Bazely, *Intermediate Accounting*, 6th ed. (Cincinnati, Ohio: South-Western Publishing Co., 1994), p. 543.

2. "Accounting for Convertible Debt and Debt Issued with Stock Purchase Warrants," *APB Opinion No. 14* (New York: AICPA, 1969), par. 12.

3. "Early Extinguishment of Debt," *Opinion of the Accounting Principles Board No. 26* (New York: AICPA, 1977).

SELECTED READINGS

"Balance Sheet Classification of Short-Term Obligations Expected to Be Refinanced." *Statement of Financial Accounting Standards No. 6.* Stamford, Conn.: FASB, 1975.

"Disclosure about Derivative Financial Instruments and Fair Value of Financial Instruments." *Statement of Financial Accounting Standards No. 119.* Norwalk, Conn.: FASB, 1994.

"Disclosure of Information about Financial Instruments with Off-Balance Sheet Risk and Financial Instruments with Concentrations of Credit Risk." *Statement of Financial Accounting Standards No. 105.* Norwalk, Conn.: FASB, 1990.

"Disclosure of Long-Term Obligations." *Statement of Financial Accounting Standards No. 47.* Stamford, Conn.: FASB, 1981.

Dukes, J. C., and H. G. Hunt III. "An Empirical Examination of Debt Covenant Restrictions and Accounting Related Debt Proxies." *Journal of Accounting and Economics* (January 1990), p. 52.

"Early Extinguishment of Debt." *Opinions of the Accounting Principles Board.* New York: AICPA, 1972.

"Elements of Financial Statements of Business Enterprises." *Statements of Financial Accounting Concepts No. 3.* Stamford, Conn.: FASB, 1980.

"Extinguishment of Debt." *Statement of Financial Accounting Standards No. 76.* Stamford, Conn.: FASB, 1983.

Forsyth, T., S. Fletcher, and R. Turpen. "Corporate Borrowing: Cash Flow Implications of In-Substance Defeasance." *The CPA Journal* (October 1994), pp. 62–63.

"Interest on Receivables and Payables." *Opinion of the Accounting Principles Board No. 21.* New York: AICPA, 1971.

Letwich, Richard. "Accounting Information in Private Market: Evidence from Private Lending Agreements." *The Accounting Review* (January 1983), pp. 23–42.

"Reporting Gains and Losses from Extinguishment of Debt." *Statement of Financial Accounting Standards No. 4.* Stamford, Conn.: FASB, 1975.

Samuelson, Richard A. "Accounting for Liabilities to Perform Services." *Accounting Horizons* (September 1993), pp. 32–45.

2

Stockholders' Equity: Contributed Capital and Retained Earnings

THE NATURE AND CHANGES IN EQUITY

The interest in this chapter is with the publicly traded corporations, owned by stockholders who have limited liability, and governed by the *articles of incorporation* or corporate charter. The capital of the firm is measured by the difference between the assets and liabilities of the firm. This difference or *residual interest* is known as the *owners' or stockholders' equity*. It is equal to the cumulative net contribution of stockholders plus the plowed-back profit. The changes in equity include:

A. Changes in equity affecting assets and liabilities which
   1. affects net income through revenues, expenses, gains or losses.
   2. affects transfers between entity and owners through investment by owners and distributions to owners.
B. Changes in equity not affecting assets or liabilities such as:
   1. Issuance of stock dividends and splits.
   2. Conversion of preferred stocks to common stocks.

Stockholders' equity is in fact the capital of the firm composed of *contributed capital* (par value of outstanding capital stock, premium less discounts on issuance, amount paid on subscription agreements, and additional assessments) and *earned capital* (plowed-back earnings). In most states, the *par value or stated value* of stock issued constitute the *legal capital.* Finally, the total corporation of stockholders' equity is as follows:

1. *Contributed Capital*
   1.a. *Capital Stock* = a designated dollar amount per share established in the articles of incorporation × number of shares outstanding.
   1.b. *Additional Paid-in-Capital* = the excess of the value over the par or stated value of the stock × number of shares outstanding.
2. *Unrealized Capital*: increases in stockholders' equity not related to the issuance of stock or to retained earnings, such as *donated capital* and *revaluation capital* (writeup or writedown of assets from cost).
3. *Retained Earnings*: income not distributed but reinvested in the firm or plowed back.

It is appropriate to note that *Additional Paid-in-Capital* is a summary account for the following transactions:

1. Discounts on capital stock issued (debit).
2. Sale of treasury stock below cost (debit).
3. Absorption of a deficit in a recapitalization (quasi-reorganization) (debit).
4. Declaration of a liquidating dividend (debit).
5. Premium on capital stock issued (credit).
6. Sale of treasury stock above cost (credit).
7. Additional capital arising in recapitalizations or revisions in the capital structure (quasi-reorganization) (credit).
8. Additional assessments on stockholders (credit).
9. Conversion of convertible bonds or preferred stock (credit).
10. Declaration of a "small" (ordinary) stock dividend (credit).

Other items may be presented as contra or adjunct equity items, generally as adjustments to or below retained earnings. Examples of the items include:

1. Foreign currency translation adjustments.
2. Unrealized holding gains and losses for available-for-sale securities.
3. Excess of additional pension liability over unrecognized prior service cost.
4. Guarantees of employee stock option plan (ESOP) debt.

5. Unearned or deferred compensation related to employee stock award plans.

6. Others.

ACCOUNTING FOR THE ISSUANCE OF CAPITAL STOCK

Various transactions are used in the issuance of capital stock. They are examined next:

Issuance of Capital Stock for Cash

When capital stock with a par value is issued for cash, the differences between the proceeds and the par value of the stock issued are accounted for as an *Additional Paid-in-Capital on Common Stock*. For example, let's assume that the Ortega Company issued 1,000 shares of its $20 par common stock for $30 per share. The entry to record the issuance is as follows:

Cash ($30 × 1,000)	30,000	
Common stock		
($20 × 1,000)		20,000
Additional Paid-in-Capital		
on Common Stock		10,000

The same entry would be used if the stock were no-par stock with a stated value of $20 (the $20 value is a minimum value below which it cannot be issued). If the stock was in fact a no-par stock, with no per-share amount printed in the stock certificate, the entry would be as follows:

Cash ($30 × 1,000)	30,000	
Common Stock–No-Par		
Value		30,000

The costs of issuing stock are either treated as a reduction of the amounts paid in (a debit to Paid-in-Capital in Excess Par) or as an organization cost to be capitalized as an intangible asset and amortized over a period not to exceed 40 years.

Issuance of Capital Stock on a Subscription Basis

Capital stock may be issued on a subscription basis, namely, on an installment basis, accounted for by a credit to *Common or Preferred Stock Subscribed* for the amount of stock the firm is obliged to issue, and a debit to *Subscription Receivable* for the amount to be collected before the subscribed stock is issued.

To illustrate, let's assume that the Albertos Company offered stocks on a subscription basis to its employees that allows them to purchase 5,000 shares of $8 per common stock at $20 per share if they put down $5 per share and pay the remaining $15 at the end of the month. The entry at the date of issuance is as follows:

Cash ($5 × 5,000)	$25,000	
Subscriptions Receivable:		
Common Stock ($15 × 5,000)	75,000	
Common Stock Subscribed		
(5,000 × 8)		$40,000
Additional Paid-in-Capital		
on Common Stock ($12 ×		
5,000)		60,000

Subscriptions Receivable may be reprinted in the current asset section of the balance sheet or as a deduction from stockholders' equity. The Securities and Exchange Commission (SEC) requires the contra-equity approach, which explains its popularity in practice.

At the end of the month, when the Albertos Company received payment for and issued 4,000 shares, the following entries are made:

Cash ($15 × 4,000)	60,000	
Subscription Receivable		60,000

and

Common Stock Subscribed	32,000	
Common stock ($8 ×		
4,000)		32,000

Assuming that the subscriber to the remaining 1,000 shares defaulted on the contract, the following entry is made:

Common Stock Subscribed		
(1,000 × $8)	8,000	
Additional Paid-in-Capital		
(1,000 × $12)	12,000	
Subscription Receivable		
(1,000 × $15)		15,000
Additional Paid-in Capital		
for Subscription Default		
(1,000 × $5)		5,000

Issuance of Capital Stock in a Nonmonetary Exchange

Capital stock may sometimes be issued for services or property other than cash. The general rule is to record the exchange at the fair market value of either the stock or the property of services, depending on whichever is readily determinable and more reliable. For example, let's assume that a corporation issued 20,000 shares of $10 par value for a patent when the stock was at $30. The transaction is recorded as follows:

Patent	600,000	
Common Stock (20,000 × $10)		200,000
Paid-in-Capital in Excess of Par (20,000 × 20)		400,000

If both the fair market value of the stock and the property of services were not easily determinable or were not reliable, the board of directors is responsible for the determination of the fair market value of the exchange. Two likely situations are: (a) an overvaluation of the property or services received resulting in an overvaluation of stockholders' equity, a phenomenon referred to as *watered stock*, or (b) an undervaluation of stockholders' equity, a phenomenon referred to as *secret reserves.*

ACCOUNTING FOR TREASURY STOCK

Treasury stock represents the stock reacquired by a firm for various reasons including the following:

1. To use for stock option, bonus, and employee purchase plans.
2. To use in the conversion of convertible preferred stocks or bonds.

3. To use excess cash and help maintain the market price of its stock.

4. To use in the acquisition of other companies.

5. To reduce the number of shares outstanding and thereby increase the earnings per share.

6. To reduce the number of shares held by outside shareholders and thereby reduce the likelihood of being acquired by another company.

7. To use for the issuance of a stock dividend.[1]

Firms may also buy back all their stock and go private, a procedure referred to as LBO (leverage buyout).

Two methods may be used to account for treasury stock: namely, (a) *the cost method*, and (b) *the par value method*. The cost method (a) accounts for the treasury stock at the reacquisition cost. When reissued, the treasury shares are credited to Paid-in-Capital from treasury stock if the reissuance price exceeds the acquisition price, and are debited to paid-in-capital from treasury stock then to retained earnings if the reissuance price is less than acquisition price. The treasury stock is reported as as deduction from total paid-in capital and retained earnings. The par value method (b) accounts for the treasury stock at the par value. At reacquisition, treasury stock at par value and paid-in-capital in excess of par are debited. Retained earnings is debited if the acquisition price is higher than the issuance price. Paid-in-capital from treasury stock is credited if the acquisition price is less than the issuance price. Finally, the treasury stock is reported as a deduction from capital stock only.

To illustrate, assume that the Share Corporation is authorized to issue 10,000 shares of $10 par common stock and entered into the following treasury stock transactions:

1. If issued, 3,000 shares of 10 par common stock at $15 per share:
   A. *Under the Cost Method and the Par Value Method*, the following entry is made:

Cash (3,000 × $15)	45,000	
Common Stock ($10 par × 3,000)		$30,000
Additional Paid-in-Capital on Common Stock ($5 × 3,000)		15,000

2. If reacquired 500 shares of common stock at $16 per share:
   A. *Under the Cost Method*

| Treasury Stock (500 × $16) | $8,000 | |
| Cash | | $8,000 |

B. *Under the Par Value Method*

Treasury Stock (500 × $10)		$5,000
Additional Paid-in-Capital		
(500 × $5)		$2,500
Retained Earnings		$500
Cash		$8,000

3. If reissued 200 shares of treasury stock at $20 per share:

A. *Under the Cost Method*

Cash (200 × $20)	$4,000	
Treasury Stock (200 × 16)		$3,200
Additional Paid-in-Capital		
on Treasury Stock		
(200 × $4)	$800	

B. *Under the Par Value Method*

Cash (200 × $20)	$4,000	
Treasury Stock		
(200 × $10)		$2,000
Additional Paid-in-Capital		
on Common Stock (200 ×		
$10)		$2,000

4. If reissued another 50 shares at $7 per share:

A. *Under the Cost Method*

Cash ($7 × 50)		$350
Additional Paid-in-Capital from		
Treasury Stock ($9 × 50)		$450
Treasury Stock (50 × $16)		$800

B. *Under the Par Value Method*

Cash (50 × $7)	$350	
Additional Paid-in-Capital in		
Common Stock	$150	
Treasury Stock (50 × $10)		$500

5. If reissued another 200 shares of treasury stock at $10 per share:

A. *Under the Cost Method*

Cash (200 × $10)	$2,000	
Additional Paid-in-Capital from		
Treasury Stock	$350	
Retained Earnings	$850	
Treasury Stock (200 ×		
$16)		$3,200

B. *Under the Par Value Method*
Cash $2,000
   Treasury Stock (200 ×
   $10) $2,000

6. If retired the last 50 shares of treasury stock:
  A. *Under the Cost Method*
  Common Stock ($10 par × 50) $500
  Additional Paid-in-Capital on
  Common Stock $250
  Retained Earnings $50
   Treasury stock (50 × $16) $800

$$\frac{\$15,000 \times 50}{3,000}$$

  B. *Under the Par Value Method*
  Common Stock, $10 par $500
   Treasury Stock
   (50 shares × $10) $500

ACCOUNTING FOR PREFERRED STOCK

Preferred stock allows the holder to have rights not available to the common stockholders. One important right is a *preference to dividends* expressed as a *percentage of par value* if the preferred stock is issued with a par value, or as a *specific dollar amount* if the preferred stock is a no-par preferred stock. Other features include the following:

Cumulative Preferred Stock

Holders of cumulative preferred stocks are owed *dividend in arrears* for years the dividend is not declared, that is, not passed. For example, holders of 5,000 shares of 10%, $100 par cumulative preferred stocks are entitled to a $10 annual dividend per share. If dividend is passed for 2 years, the preferred shareholders are entitled to dividend in arrears of $100,000 ($10 × 5,000 shares × 2 years) and $50,000 for the third year. The amount paid in the third year is $150,000.

Participating Preferred Stock

Holders of participating preferred stock are entitled to share either fully (fully participating preferred stock) or partially (partially participating preferred stock) in any dividend available after the preferred stockholders have been paid at a rate equal to that paid for preferred stock. If preferred stock is paid at 10%, any amount in excess of 10% paid to common shareholders is shared between the preferred and common stockholders.

Convertible Preferred Stock

Holders of convertible preferred stock have the option to exchange their preferred shares for a specified number of common stock.

Callable Preferred Stock

Callable preferred stock allows the corporation to call or redeem at its option the outstanding preferred shares under conditions specified by the stock contract. At issuance of the callable preferred stock, the difference between the market and par value is credited to the additional Paid-in-Capital on Preferred Stock. At recall, the difference is not treated as a gain or loss and two situations arise:

A. If the call price exceeds the contributed capital (preferred stock plus additional paid-in-capital associated with the recalled preferred stock), the difference or "loss" is debited to retained earnings like a dividend distribution.

B. If the call price is less than the contributed capital, the difference or "gain" is credited to Additional Paid-in-Capital from Recall of Preferred Stock.

For example, let's assume that the XYZ Corporation has 5,000 shares of $100 par callable preferred stock issued at $120 per share.

A. Assuming a call price of $130, the following entry is made at the recall:

Preferred Stock ($100 par × 5,000)	500,000	
Additional Paid-in-Capital or Preferred Stock	100,000	
Retained Earnings ($650,000 − $600,000)	50,000	
Cash ($130 × 5,000)		650,000

B. Assuming a call price of $110, the following entry is made at recall:

Preferred Stock, $100 par	500,000	

Additional Paid-in-Capital on Preferred Stock	100,000	
Cash ($110 × 5,000)		550,000
Additional Paid-in-Capital from Recall of Preferred Stock ($600,000 − $550,000)		50,000

Preferred Stock with Stock Warrants

Preferred stocks may be issued with stock warrants offering the holder not only preference as to dividends but also rights to purchase additional shares of common stock at a specified price over some future period. Given these dual rights the proceeds from the issuance of preferred stock with attachable warrants are to be allocated to preferred stockholders' equity and common stockholders' equity, on the basis of the relative fair values of the two securities at the time of issuance. To illustrate, let's assume that the XYZ Company issues 5,000 shares of $100 par value preferred stock at a price of $130 per share with a detachable warrant that allows the holder to purchase for each preferred share one share of $20 par common stock at $50 per share. Following the issuance, the preferred stock was selling ex-rights (without the warrants) at a market price of $120, while the warrant was selling for $8 each. The following computations are required:

1. Market Value of Preferred Stock: ($120 × 5,000)   = $600,000
2. Market Value of Warrants: ($8 × 5,000)   = $40,000
3. Total Market Value: ($600,000 + 40,000)   = $640,000
4. Issuance Value ($130 × 5,000)   = $650,000
5. Allocation to Preferred Stock: = $609,375
   $650,000 × $600,000
   $640,000
6. Allocation to Warrants: = $40,625
   $650,000 × $40,000
   $640,000

At the time of issuance the following entry is made:

Cash ($130 × 5,000)   650,000

Preferred Stock, $100 par		
(5,000 × $100)		500,000
Additional Paid-in-Capital		
on Preferred Stock		109,375
Common Stock Warrants		40,625

When the warrants are exercised, the following entry is made:

Cash ($5,000 × $50)	250,000	
Common Stock Warrants	40,625	
Common Stock, $20 par		100,000
Additional Paid-in-Capital		
on Common Stock		190,625

RETAINED EARNINGS

Notice the following basic accounting equations:

$$\text{Assets} = \text{liabilities} + \text{owners' equity} + \text{retained earnings}$$

$$\text{Net Profit} = \text{Revenues} - \text{Expenses}$$

From the two equations, retained earnings appears as the main link between the balance sheet and profit equations. Retained Earnings is subject to increases or credits and decreases or debits.

Some of the increases in debits include:

1. Net income.
2. Prior period adjustments.
3. Adjustments due to quasi-reorganization.

Some of the decreases or debits include:

1. Loss.
2. Prior period adjustments and certain changes in accounting principles.
3. Cash or scrip dividends.
4. Property dividends.
5. Some treasury earning stock transactions.

ACCOUNTING FOR DIVIDENDS

As stated earlier, the decrease in retained earnings follows the distribution of dividends. The types of dividends include (1) cash, (2) property, (3) scrip, (4) liquidating, and (5) stock. With the exception of stock dividends, all the other dividends reduce the stockholders' equity in the corporation.

Cash Dividends

Firms distribute as cash dividends a certain percentage of annual earnings in payout rates. Four dates are crucial to accounting for cash dividends as follows:

1. The *date of declaration* is the date a resolution to pay cash dividends to *stockholders of record* on a specific future date is approved by the board of directors. At that date the firm incurs a liability prompting the recognition of a short-term debt—Dividends Payable and the debit to either Retained Earnings or Cash Dividend Declared.
2. The *ex-dividend date* is the date the stock stops selling with dividends attached. The period between the date of declaration and the ex-dividend date is used by the firm to update its stockholders' ledger.
3. The *date of record* is the date at which the stockholders figuring in the stockholders' ledger are entitled to the cash dividend. No entry is required.
4. The *date of payment* is the date at which the firm distributes the dividend checks and eliminates the dividend payable as a liability.

For example, let's assume that the Natsumura Corporation, on March 15, 1996, declared a cash dividend of $1 per share on 2,000,000 shares payable June 1, 1996, to all stockholders of record April 15. The following entries are required:

1. Date of declaration, March 15, 1996.

Retained Earnings (Cash Dividend Declared)	2,000,000	
Dividends Payable		2,000,000

2. Date of record, April 15, 1996.
   Memorandum entry that the firm will pay a dividend to all stockholders of record as of today, the date of record.

3. Date of payment, June 1, 1996.

Dividends Payable	2,000,000	
Cash		2,000,000

It is appropriate to note that cash dividend declared is closed at year-end to Retained Earnings.

Property Dividends

Firms may elect to declare a property dividend that is payable in non-monetary assets rather than declaring a cash dividend. Because a property dividend can be classified as a *nonreciprocal nonmonetary transfer to owners*, the property distributed is restated at fair market value at the date of declaration and a gain or loss is recognized.

For example, let's assume that the ABC Corporation declares a property dividend, payable in bonds of company XYZ being held to maturity and costing $500,000. At the date of declaration the bonds had a market value of $600,000. The following entries are required:

A. Date of Declaration

Investments in Company XYZ Bonds	100,000	
Gain on Appreciation of Bonds		100,000
($600,000 − $500,000)		
Retained Earnings (Property Dividend Declared)		$600,00
Property Dividends Payable		$600,000

B. Date of Distribution

Property Dividends Payable	600,000	
Investments in Company XYZ Bonds		600,000

Scrip Dividends

Firms may find themselves with sufficient retained earnings to declare a dividend but not enough liquidity for distribution. In such case, firms may elect to declare a scrip dividend—dividend payable in scrip—by issuing promissory notes requiring them to pay the dividends at a later date. The accounting treatment at the date of declaration consists of debiting retained earnings or scrip dividends declared and crediting notes payable to stockholders or scrip dividend payable. At the date of distribution, the firm debits the note payable or scrip payable, and the related interest expense and credit cash. For example, let's assume that the Bannos Company declared, on June 17, 1996, a scrip dividend in the form of a three-month promissory note amount to $1 a share on 3,000,000 shares outstanding. The interest rate on the notes is 10% per year. The following entries are required:

1. At the date of declaration, June 17, 1996
    Retained Earnings (Scrip
    Dividends Declared)   3,000,000
        Notes Payable to
        Stockholders (Scrip
        Dividends Payable)   3,000,000
        ($1 × 3,000,000)

2. At the date of payment, September 17, 1996
    Note Payable to Stockholders   3,000,000
    Interest Expense   75,000
    ($3,000,000 × .10 × 3/12)
        Cash   3,075,000

Liquidating Dividends

Dividends paid based on other than retained earnings are called liquidating dividends, as a return of contributed capital rather than a distribution of retained earnings. They are treated as a reduction of contributed capital, either additional paid-in-capital or a special contra-contributed capital account, designated as Contributed Capital Distributed as a Liquidating Dividend.

For example, let's assume that the Weigandt Company issued dividend to its common stockholders of $2,500,000 of which $1,000,000 is considered income and the rest a return of contributed capital. The following entries are required:

A. At the date of declaration
    Retained Earnings   1,000,000
    Additional Paid-in-Capital   1,500,000

Dividends Payable		2,500,000

B. At the date of payment

Dividends Payable	2,500,000	
Cash		2,500,000

Stock Dividends

A firm with adequate retained earnings but insufficient liquidity may elect to issue stock dividends by a pro rate distribution of additional shares of the firm's own stock to its stockholders. The transaction is made by a capitalization of retained earnings resulting in a reduction of retained earnings and an increase in some contributed capital accounts. No corporate assets are distributed; the value of the total stockholders' equity remains unchanged as well as each stockholder's percentage ownership in the firm. Accounting for stock dividends differs depending on the size of the issue:

A. For *small stock dividend*, that is less than 20–25% of the common shares outstanding at the time of the dividend declaration, *fair market value* is used to capitalize retained earnings and an increase in capital stock and additional paid-in-capital.

B. For *large stock dividend*, that is more than 20–25% of the common shares outstanding at the time of the dividend declaration, *par value* is issued to capitalize retained earnings resulting in a reduction of retained earnings and an increase in capital stock.

To illustrate the accounting for small stock dividend, let's assume a corporation that has the following stockholders' equity prior to the issuance of a small stock dividend:

Common Stock, $20 par (30,000 shares issued and outstanding)	$600,000
Additional Paid-in-Capital	300,000
Retained Earnings	600,000
Total Stockholders' Equity	$1,500,000

Let's also assume that the firm issued a 20% stock dividend on a date where the stock was selling at $25 per share. The fair value of the 6,000 shares is $150,000. The following entries are required:

A. At the date of declaration

Retained Earnings	150,000	
Common Stock Dividend		
Distributable	120,000	
Additional Paid-in-Capital		
from Stock Dividend		30,000

B. At the date of issuance

Common Stock Dividend		
Distribution	120,000	
Common Stock, $20 par		120,000

Following the issuance the stockholders' equity is as follows:

Common Stock, $20 par	$720,000
(36,000 shares issued and	
outstanding)	
Additional Paid-in-Capital	330,000
Retained Earnings	450,000
Total Stockholders' Equity	$1,500,000

Let's now assume that the firm issued instead a 50% stock dividend. The following entries are required at the time of declaration.

Retained Earnings (50% ×		
30,000 share × $20)	300,000	
Common Stock Dividend		
Distributable		300,000

At the time of distribution the following entry is required:

Common Stock Dividend		
Distributable	300,000	
Common Stock, $20 par		300,000

Following the issuance the stockholders' equity is as follows:

Common Stock, $20 par	
(45,000)	$900,000
Additional Paid-in-Capital	300,000
Retained Earnings	300,000
Total Stockholders' Equity	1,500,000

Note that the large stock dividend is treated as a stock split, that is, *a split-up effected in the form of a dividend*. In fact, for a stock split no entry is required except a memorandum to notice the increase in the number of shares and the decrease in the par value. For example, a 2-for-1 split of $6,000 shares at $10 par value results in a common stock of $16,000 shares at $5 par value.

APPROPRIATIONS OF RETAINED EARNINGS

To issue that the retained earnings may be used for more than the declaration and the payment of dividends, firms may appropriate (restrict) retained earnings, "provided that it is shown within the stockholders' equity section of the balance sheet and is clearly identified as an appropriation of retained earnings."[2] The appropriation may be motivated by (a) legal restriction, (b) contractual restrictions, (c) existence of possible or expected loss, and (d) protection of working capital position.[3] Note, however, that FASB Statement No. 5 clearly states that "Costs or losses shall not be charged to an appropriation of retained earnings, and no part of the appropriation shall be transferred to income."[4]

To illustrate the formal entries associated with appropriation of retained earnings, let's assume that the XYZ Company is required by a debt covenant that an appropriation for sinking fund or appropriation for bond indebtedness is to be created by transfer from retained earnings of $500,000 a year for the 10-year life of the bonds. Therefore the entry for each year is:

Retained Earnings	500,000	
Retained Earnings		
Appropriated for Sinking		
Fund		500,000

At the end of 10 years and assuming the bonds are retired, the following entry is required:

Retained Earnings Appropriated		
for Sinking Fund	500,000	
Retained Earnings		500,000

NOTES

1. Loren A. Nikolai and John D. Bazley, *Intermediate Accounting*, 6th ed. (Cincinnati, Ohio: South-Western Publishing Co., 1994), p. 852.

2. "Accounting for Contingencies," *FASB Statement of Financial Accounting Standards No. 5* (Stamford, Conn.: FASB, 1975), par. 15.

3. Donald E. Kieso and Jerry J. Weygandt, *Intermediate Accounting*, 4th ed. (New York: John Wiley & Sons, 1995), p. 786.

4. "Accounting for Contingencies," par. 15.

3

Investments

INTRODUCTION

Firms buy bonds and stocks to generate investment revenues and dividend revenues as well as for speculative reasons. The different objectives for these investments dictate different accounting treatments to insure a fair reporting. Accordingly, this chapter examines the conventional accounting treatments for investments in both debt securities and equity securities.

TYPES OF INVESTMENTS IN DEBT SECURITIES

Investments in debt securities and investments in equity securities that have readily determinable fair values are the subject of FASB Statement No. 115. Three types of securities are presented:

1. *Debt Securities Held to Maturity*: The firm has the positive interest and ability to hold those securities to maturity.
2. *Trading Securities*: They are acquired and held for the sole purpose of generating short-term income through sale.
3. *Securities Available-for-Sale*: They are securities that are not classified as either debt securities held to maturity or trading securities.

At the time of acquisition each of these types of securities is accounted for at cost with the income statement including dividend revenue, interest revenue and realized holdings gains and losses. The subsequent valuation in the balance sheet and the recognition of unrealized holdings gains and losses differ, however, as follows:

1. Debt securities held to maturity, valued at their *amortized* cost, that is, the acquisition cost after amortization of any premium or discount each period as interest revenue is recognized. Therefore, no unrealized holdings gains or losses are recognized.
2. Trading securities are valued at their *fair value* on the balance sheet date which leads to the recognition of unrealized holdings gains and losses in the income statement.
3. Securities available for sale are valued at fair value on the balance sheet date which leads to the recognition of unrealized holdings gains and losses as a separate component of stockholders' equity until realized.

ACCOUNTING FOR INVESTMENTS IN DEBT SECURITIES

Investments in Debt Securities Held to Maturity

As stated earlier, investments in debt securities held to maturity are valued at cost at the time of acquisition, then subsequently at amortized cost. Any premium or discount is amortized over the remaining life of the bonds, thereby allocating the proper amount of revenue to each period. Let's illustrate both the situations of premium and discount.

Situation 1: Case of a Premium

Let's assume that the Jackson Company purchased, on January 1, 1996, investments in bonds to be held to maturity with a face value of $200,000 of five-year bonds paying semi-annual interest with a stated rate of 12% and an effective interest rate of 10% for $215,443.42. On January 1, 1996, the Jackson Company makes the following entry:

```
Investments in Debt Securities
Held to Maturity              $215,443.42
    Cash                                      215,443.42
```

Exhibit 3.1 shows the schedule for computing interest revenue and premium amortization using the effective interest method. On June 30, 1996, the first interest receipt is recorded as follows:

Exhibit 3.1
Jackson Company: Schedule of Bond Premium Amortization, Effective Interest Method, Semi-Annual Interest Payments, 12% Bond Sold to Yield 10%

Date	Cash Received (a)	Interest Revenue (b)	Investment in Debt Securities (c)	Carrying Value of Investment in Debt Securities (d)
1/01/96				$215,443.42
6/30/96	$12,000	$10,772.17	$1,227.83	214,215.59
12/31/97	12,000	10,710.77	1,289.22	212,926.37
6/30/97	12,000	10,646.31	1,353.68	211,572.69
12/31/97	12,000	10,578.63	1,421.36	210,151.33
6/30/98	12,000	10,507.56	1,492.43	208,658.90
12/31/98	12,000	10,432.94	1,567.05	207,091.85
6/30/99	12,000	10,354.59	1,645.40	205,446.45
12/31/99	12,000	10,272.32	1,727.67	203,718.78
6/30/00	12,000	10,185.93	1,814.06	201,904.72
12/31/00	12,000	10,095.23	1,904.76	200,000.00

(a) $200,000 (face value) × 0.12 (stated rate) × ½ year
(b) Previous book value × 0.10 (effective rate) × ½ year
(c) (a) − (b)
(d) Previous book value − (c)

Cash	$12,000	
Investments in Debt Securities Held to Maturity		1,227.83
Interest Revenue		10,710.77

Situation 2: Case of a Discount

Let's assume that the Jackson Company purchased, on January 1, 1996, $200,000 of five-year bonds paying semi-annual interest rate with a

Exhibit 3.2
Jackson Company: Schedule of Bond Discount Amortization, Effective Interest Method, Semi-Annual Interest Payments, 12% Bonds Sold to Yield 14%

Date	Cash Received (a)	Interest Revenue (b)	Discount Amortized (c)	Carrying Value of Bonds (d)
1/01/96				$185,952.78
6/30/96	$12,000	$13,016.69	$1,016.69	186,969.47
12/31/96	12,000	13,087.86	1,087.86	188,057.33
6/30/97	12,000	13,164.01	1,164.01	189,221.34
12/31/97	12,000	13,245.49	1,254.43	190,466.83
6/30/98	12,000	13,332.67	1,332.67	191,799.50
12/31/98	12,000	13,425.96	1,425.96	193,225.46
6/30/99	12,000	13,525.78	1,525.78	194,751.24
12/31/99	12,000	13,632.58	1,632.58	196,751.24
6/30/00	12,000	13,746.86	1,746.86	198,130.68
12/31/00	12,000	13,869.14	1,869.14	200,000.00

(a) $200,000 (face value) × 0.12 (stated rate) × ½ year
(b) Previous book value × 0.14 (effective rate) × ½ year
(c) (b)− (a)
(d) Previous book value + (c)

stated rate of 12% and an effective rate of 14% for $185,952.78. On January 1, 1996, the Jackson Company makes the following entry:

```
Investments in Debt Securities
  Held to Maturity              185,952.78
       Cash                                  185,952.78
```

Exhibit 3.2 illustrates the schedule for computing the interest revenue and the discount amortization. On June 30, 1996, the first interest receipt is recorded as follows:

Cash	12,000	
Investments in Debt Securities		
Held to Maturity	1,016.69	
Interest Revenue		13,016.69

Let's assume that on November 1, 2000, the Jackson Company sells the investment at 99 ¾ plus interest. The discount amortization from July 1, 2000 until November 1, 2000 is $1,246.09 (1,869.14 × 4/6). This amortization is recognized on November 1, 2000 as follows:

Investments in Debt Securities		
Held to Maturity	1,246.09	
Interest Revenue		1,264.09

Therefore the gain or loss on the rate is computed as follows:

A. Book Value of the Bonds on November 1, 2000
   1. Amortized Cost, July 1, 2000 = $198,130.68
   2. Plus: Discount Amortization up
      until November 1, 2000 =   1,246.09
   3. Book Value   199,376.77
B. Selling Price of Bonds   199,500.00
C. Gain on Sale of Bonds ($199,500 −
   $199,376.77)   123.23

Therefore, the following entry to record the sale is made on November 1, 2000.

Cash	207,500	
Interest Revenue ($12,000		
× 4/6)		8,000.00
Investments in Debt		
Securities Held to Maturity		199,376.77
Gain in Sale of Securities		123.23

Investments in Available-for-Sale Securities

As stated earlier, investments in available-for-sale securities are recorded at cost at acquisition, then are reported at fair value in balance sheet date, with the unrealized gains and losses accounted for as a separate contra-account to stockholders' equity until realized. To illustrate, let's assume that the Dodd Company purchased, on January 1, 1996, investments in bonds available-for-sale with a face value of $200,000 of five-year bonds paying semi-annual interest rate of 10% for $215,443.42. On May 1, 1996, the Dodd Company includes the following entry:

Investments in Securities		
Available-for-Sale	215,443.42	
Cash		215,443.42

Exhibit 3.1 shows the schedule for computing interest revenue and premium amortization using the effective interest method. On June 30, 1996, the following interest revenue entry is made:

Cash	12,000	
Investments in Securities		
Available-for-Sale		1,227.83
Interest Revenue		10,710.77

Similarly, on December 31, 1996, the following entry is made to recognize interest revenue

Interest Receivable	12,000	
Investments in Securities		
Available-for-Sale		1,289.22
Interest Revenue		10,710.77

Let's assume that the fair value of the bonds at year-end is $210,000. Therefore the Dodd Company needs to recognize a $2,926.37 unrealized holdings loss ($210,000−$212,986.37) as follows:

Unrealized Holdings Gain or		
Loss-Equity	2,926.37	
Securities Fair Value		
Adjustment		2,926.37

The Securities Fair Value Adjustment (or Allowance for Change in Value of Investment) is an adjunct/contra to the investment in Securities Available-for-Sale, and the Unrealized Holdings Gain or Loss-Equity is an adjunct/contra account to the stockholder's equity account.

Let's assume that the Dodd Company sells the bonds at the end of 1997 for $200,000, the corporation of the realized loss is as follows:

Amortized Cost of Bonds	$210,151.33
Less: Selling Price of Bonds	200,000.00
Loss on Sale of Bonds	$10,151.33

The sale is recorded as follows:

Cash		200,000
Security Fair Value Adjustment		2,926.37
Loss or Sale of Securities	10,151.33	
Unrealized Holdings Gain or Loss-Equity		2,926.37
Investment in Securities Available-for-Sale		210,151.33

Trading Securities

As stated earlier, trading securities are acquired at cost and valued subsequently at fair value. Unlike in the case of available-for-sale securities, the unrealized holdings gains or losses are recognized as part of net income. For example, let's assume that the Ram Company had a portfolio of bonds with, at the end of the year, a cost $600,000 and a fair value of $610,000. The following entry will be used to record the unrealized holdings gain:

Securities Fair Value Adjustment (Trading)	$10,000	
Unrealized Holdings Gain or Loss-Income		10,000

INVESTMENTS IN EQUITY SECURITIES

The accounting for investments in equity securities depends on the percentage of ownership the investor has in the stock of another firm (the investee). Three types of situations are probable:

1. The investor holds less than 20% and therefore has passive interest. The *fair value method* is to be used.

2. The investor holds between 20% and 50% and therefore has significant influence. The *equity method* is to be used.

3. The investor holds more than 50% and therefore has controlling interest. *Consolidation* is to be used.

The Case of Holdings Less than 20%

In the case of holdings less than 20%, the fair value method is to be used for both available-for-sale equity securities and trading equity securities. They are examined next.

Available-for-Sale Securities

To illustrate, let's assume that on October 3, 1996, the Dyden Company purchased $560,000 worth of shares in the XYZ Company, amounting to less than 20% interest. The following entry is made at the date of purchase:

Investments in Available-for-Sale Securities	$560,000	
Cash		560,000

On December 3, 1996, the Dyden Company received a cash dividend of $5,000 from the XYZ investment. The following entry is made:

Cash	$5,000	
Dividend Revenue		5,000

Note that the Dyden Company does not recognize its share of the income of the XYZ but only the cash dividends received.

On December 31, 1996, the fair value of the investment is found to be equal to $500,000. The following entry is made:

Unrealized Holdings Gain or Loss-Equity	$60,000	
Securities Fair Value Adjustment		60,000

Trading Securities

Accounting for trading securities when holdings are less than 20% is similar for accounting for available-for-sale securities, except that the unrealized holdings gain or loss is reported part of net income as unrealized holdings gain or loss-income.

The Case of Holdings between 20% and 50%

As stated earlier, in the case of holdings between 20% and 50%, the investor may be presumed to have the ability to exercise significant influence over operating and financial policies of the investee.[1] Accordingly, in such a case Accounting Principles Board Opinion No. 18 requires the use of the equity method. However, FASB Interpretation No. 35 provides some examples where holdings between 20% and 50% may not allow the exercise of *significant influence* and the investee should not use the equity method. These cases are the following:

1. The investee is opposed to the investor's purchase of its stock by filing a complaint with governmental regulatory authorities or filing a suit against the investor.
2. The investor and the investee sign an agreement under which the investor surrenders important shareholder rights.
3. A small group of investors operate the firm without regard to the views of the investor, thereby limiting his/her "significant influence."
4. The investor needs or wants more financial information than is made available by the investee, tries to obtain it and fails.
5. The investor tries and fails to obtain representation on the investee's board of directors.[2]

The Equity Method versus the Fair Value Method

Under the equity method, the investment in common stock is initially recorded at cost, then is increased (decreased) by the investor's share of investee income (loss) and decreased by all dividends received from the investee. In other words,

$$Investment = \text{Acquisition Cost} + \text{Investor's Share of Investee}$$
$$\text{Income} - \text{Dividends Received}$$

where

$$Investor's\ Share\ of\ Investee\ Income = (\text{Investee's Net Income}$$
$$\times \text{Percentage of Ownership}) - \text{Adjustments}$$

and

$$Dividends\ Received = (\text{Total Dividends Paid by the Investee} \\ \times \text{Percentage of Ownership})$$

To illustrate the differences between the equity method and the fair value method, let's assume the following example:

1. On November 2, 1996, the XYZ Company acquired 5,000 shares (30% of the ABC Company common stock) at a cost of $20 a share.
   A. *Under the fair value method* (assuming no significant influence)

Available-for-Sale Securities	100,000	
Cash		100,000

   B. *Under the equity method* (assuming significant influence)

Investment in ABC Stock	100,000	
Cash		100,000

2. In 1996 the XYZ Company reported a net income of $100,000.
   A. Under the fair value method: No entry is required.
   B. Under the equity method:

Investment in ABC Stock		
($100,000 × 30%)	30,000	
Revenue from Investment		30,000

3. At the end of the year 1996, the fair value of ABC stock was $30 per share.
   A. Under the equity method: No entry is required.
   B. Under the fair value method:

Securities Fair Value Adjustment		
[($30 − $20)] × 5,000	50,000	
Unrealized Holdings Gain or Loss-Equity		50,000

4. On February 1, 1997, the ABC Company paid a total cash dividend of $50,000.
   A. Under the fair value method:

Cash	15,000	
Dividend Revenue ($50,000 × 30%)		15,000

B. Under the equity method:

Cash		15,000
Investment in ABC Stock		15,000

5. In 1997, the ABC Company reported a $100,000 loss.
   A. Under the fair value method: No entry is required.
   B. Under the equity method:

Loss on Investment	30,000	
Investment in ABC Stock		
($100,000 × 30%)		30,000

6. At the end of 1997, the fair value of the ABC stock was $15 per share.
   A. Under the equity method: No entry is required.
   B. Under the fair value method:

Unrealized Holdings Gain or Loss-		
Equity ($20 − $15)	25,000	
Securities Fair Value		
Adjustment		25,000

Under the equity method, there is a need not only to periodically change the value of the investment account for the increases and decreases in the investor's proportionate share of income and decreases for dividends received, but also the need to amortize the difference between the investor's initial acquisition cost and the investor's proportional share of the underlying book value of the investee at the date of purchase.

To illustrate, assume that the Dole Company purchases, on January 1, 1996, 30% of the 100,000 shares of the Monti Company for $200,000. On the date of acquisition the following information of the Monti Company was available:

	Book Value	Fair Market Value
Depreciable Assets (remaining life, 10 years)	$500,000	$550,000
Other New Depreciable Assets	100,000	150,000
Total	$600,000	$700,000

Liabilities	$100,000
Common Stock	$250,000

Retained Earnings $250,000
Total $600,000

The Monti Company paid, on June 15, 1996, a cash dividend of $30,000 and reported net income of $90,000 and an extraordinary gain of $20,000. The Dole Company will make the following entries:

1. To record the purchase of 30,000 shares for $200,000 on January 1, 1996.

Investment in Monti Stock	$200,000	
Cash		200,000

2. To record the dividend received of $9,000 ($30,000 × 30%) on June 15, 1996.

Cash	9,000	
Investment in Monti Stock		9,000

3. To record share of Monti Company's ordinary and extraordinary income, on December 31, 1996.

Investment in Monti Stock	33,000	
Revenue from Investment (ordinary) ($90,000 × 30%)		27,000
Gain from Investment (extraordinary) ($20,000 × 30%)		6,000

4. To depreciate the proportionate share of any difference between the fair market and book value of investee depreciable assets.

Revenue from Investment (ordinary)	$1,500	
Investment in Monti Stock		1,500

The excess of fair market value over book value of assets at the time of acquisition was $50,000 ($550,000 − $500,000). The Dole Company's share is $15,000 ($50,000 × 30%). The share per year is $1,500 (15,000/10).

5. To depreciate goodwill

Revenue from Investment (ordinary)	$750	
Investment in Monti Stock		$750

The goodwill at the time of acquisition is computed as follows:

1. Purchase Price

$200,000

2. Book Value of Net Asset Acquired
   [30% ($600,000 − $100,000)] $150,000

3. Adjustments:
   A. Increase in depreciable assets
   [30% ($550,000 − $500,000)]   15,000

   B. Increase in other depreciable
   assets [30% ($150,000 −
   $100,000)]   15,000

4. Fair Market Value of Assets Acquired

(180,000)

5. Purchased Goodwill

20,000

Assuming goodwill is amortized over 20 years, the yearly change is $750 ($15,000/20).

NOTES

1. "The Equity Method of Accounting for Investments in Common Stock," *Opinion of Accounting Principles Board No. 18* (New York: AICPA, 1971), par. 17.

2. Ibid.

4

Accounting for Income Taxes

INTRODUCTION

Generally Accepted Accounting Principles (GAAP) are issued for the conduct of financial accounting and the computation of *Pretax Financial Income* or income for book purpose. The Internal Revenue Code (IRC) rules are used for the conduct of income tax reporting and the computation of *Taxable Income* or income for tax purposes, from which the firm's tax payable is derived. The differences between pretax financial income and taxable income (and therefore between income tax expense and income tax payable) fall in the following five categories:

1. Permanent differences,
2. Temporary differences,
3. Operating loss carrybacks and carryforwards,
4. Tax credits, and
5. Intraperiod tax allocation.

As a result of these differences, the accountant needs to determine (a) the current and noncurrent income tax liabilities and/or assets to be reported in the balance sheet and (b) the income tax expense to be deducted from the pretax financial income in the income statement. The problem is known as accounting for income tax allocation, and is the subject of this chapter. It is based on FASB Statement No. 109, entitled "Accounting for Income Taxes."[1]

TEMPORARY DIFFERENCES

Interperiod income tax allocation deals with the allocation of the firm's tax obligation as an expense to various periods. It is required because of temporary differences between pretax financial income and taxable income in a given period that will *reverse* in a later period. They are *timing* differences because they affect pretax financial income and taxable income in different periods. Two results are:

1. A *deferred tax liability* is the increase in taxes payable in future years as a result of *taxable temporary differences* existing at the end of the current year.
2. A *deferred tax asset* is the increase in taxes refundable (or saved) in future years as a result of *deductible temporary differences* existing at the end of the current year.

Examples of temporary differences include:

A. *Differences between financial accounting income and tax income.*
   A1. *Revenues or gains are included in pretax financial income before being included in taxable income.* Examples include:
      A1.1. *Gross profit on installment sales* recognized at a point of sale for financial reporting (accrual basis) but at the time of collection for income tax purposes (cash basis).
      A1.2. *Gross profit on long-term contracts* recognized under the percentage-of-completion method for financial reporting and the percentage-of-completion capitalized cost method for income tax purposes (portion of related gross profit deferred for tax purposes).
      A1.3. *Investment income* recognized under the equity method for financial reporting and the cost method for tax purposes (as dividends are received).
      A1.4. *Gain or involuntary conversion of nonmonetary asset* recognized for financial reporting but deferred for tax purposes.
   A2. *Revenues or gains are included in taxable income before being included in accounting income.* Examples include:
      A2.1. *Rent, interest, royalties and subscription received in advance* are taxable when received and recognized in financial reporting only when the service is provided.

    A2.2. *Gains on sales and leasebacks* are taxable at the date of sale but deferred over the life of the lease contract for financial reporting.

  A3. *Expenses or losses are deducted for income tax purposes before they are deducted to compute pretax financial income.* Examples include:

    A3.1. *Depreciable assets are depreciated* for income tax purposes over the prescribed tax life by (a) an accelerated method if purchased before 1981, (b) an Accelerated Cost Recovery System (ACRS) if purchased between 1981 and 1986 and (c) a Modified Accelerated Cost Recovery System (MACRS) if purchased after 1986, and for financial reporting by a financial reporting method over a longer period.

    A3.2. *Prepaid expenses, taxes and interest on self-construction projects* are deducted on the tax return when paid and capitalized for financial reporting.

  A4. *Expenses or losses are deducted to compute pretax financial income before being deducted for income tax purposes.* Examples include:

    A4.1. *Product warranty costs, bad debts, and losses on inventories* are expensed in the current year for financial reporting and deducted as actually incurred in a later period to compute taxable income.

    A4.2. *Contingent liabilities* are expressed for financial reporting when a loss is profitable and measurable, and are deductible for tax purposes when they are actually paid.[2]

B. *Direct adjustments to book or tax assets and liabilities that cause a difference between book and tax basis of assets and liabilities.* Examples include:

  B1. Reduction in the tax basis of depreciable assets because of an investment credit accounted for by the deferred method. Basically, a full investment tax credit (ITC) is taken by an entity and the tax basis of assets is reduced by ½ of ITC under Tax Act of 1982.

  B2. A reduction in the tax basis of depreciable assets because of other tax credits, like the deferral method used for ITC under Opinion No. 2. Basically, the financial basis of assets is reduced by ITC.

  B3. An increase in the tax basis of assets because of indexing whenever the local currency is the functional currency. The indexing for inflation when local currency is functional currency causes the tax basis of asset to increase.

  B4. Business combinations accounted for by the purchase method where tax and financial basis of assets and/or liabilities are different. The revaluation of financial assets and/or liabilities may cause differences between financial basis and tax basis.

PERMANENT DIFFERENCES

Differences between pretax financial income and taxable income in a given period that *will never reverse* in a later period are permanent differences. They affect either pretax financial income or tax income but not both, as a result of tax law provisions enacted by Congress to implement a given economic policy. These permanent differences do not lead to the recognition of any deferred taxes. Examples of permanent differences include:

A. *Revenues that are recognized for financial reporting but never for tax purposes.* Examples include:
   A1. *Interest received on state and municipal bonds* where the IRC provides that it is not a taxable revenue.
   A2. *Proceeds from life insurance upon the death of an insured employee* are not considered taxable revenue of the IRC.
B. *Examples that are recognized for financial reporting but never for tax purposes.* Examples include:
   B1. *Life insurance premiums on key officers or employees* are not deductible for tax purposes.
   B2. *Various expenses* that include (a) compensation expense linked to certain employee stock options, (b) fine and expenses resulting from a violation of the law and (c) expenses needed to obtain tax-exempt income.
C. *Deductions that are allowed for tax purposes but are not expensed for financial reporting.* Examples include:
   C1. Percentage depletion of natural resources in excess of cost depletion used to motivate exploration for natural resources.
   C2. *Special deduction for dividends from U.S. corporations*, generally 70 to 80%, is allowed by the IRC.

CONCEPTUAL ISSUES

The *first conceptual issue* is whether firms should be required to make interperiod income tax allocation for temporary differences or proceed with no interperiod tax allocation where the income tax expense is just equal to the current income tax obligation. Given that the two recognized objectives of accounting for income taxes are (a) to recognize the amount of tax obligation or refund of a firm for the current year, and (b) to recognize deferred tax liabilities and assets for the future tax consequences of events recognized by either financial accounting or tax accounting, the answer to the first conceptual issue is to *require interperiod tax allocation of temporary differences.*

The *second conceptual issue* is whether the interperiod tax allocation be based on the partial or comprehensive recognition approach. *Partial recognition* argues for the recognition of deferred tax consequences of *only* those temporary differences that are not recurring and are expected to reverse in a relatively short time period. *Comprehensive recognition* argues for the recognition of the deferred tax consequences of all the temporary differences. Given that accounting for the tax consequences of temporary differences should not be based on assumption relating to future offsetting temporary differences for future events not yet recognized in the financial statements, the answer to the second conceptual issue is to *require a comprehensive allocation approach.*

The *third conceptual issue* is whether the allocation should be based on the *asset/liability method* (based on enacted future tax rates), the *deferred method* (based on originality tax rates), or the *net of tax method.* The FASB opted in FASB No. 109 for the asset/liability method as the most consistent method for accounting for income taxes. To implement these objectives, the FASB provided for basic principles to be applied in accounting for income taxes at the date of the firm's financial statements:

1. A current tax liability or asset is recognized for the estimated tax obligation or refund on its income tax return for the current year.
2. A deferred tax liability or asset is recognized for the estimated future tax effects of each temporary difference and carryforwards.
3. The measurement of current and deferred tax liabilities is based on provisions of the enacted tax law; the effects of future changes in tax laws or rates are not anticipated.
4. The measurement of deferred tax assets is reduced, if necessary, by the amount of any tax benefits that, based on available evidence, are not expected to be realized.[3]

The end result may be summarized as follows:

Thus, under generally accepted accounting principles, interperiod income tax allocation is used to determine the deferred taxes and liabilities for all temporary differences, based on the currently enacted income tax rates and laws that will be in existence when the temporary differences result in future taxable amounts or deductible amounts. The deferred tax assets and liabilities are adjusted when changes in the income tax rates are enacted.[4]

COMPARISON OF THE THREE DIFFERENT METHODS OF TAX ALLOCATION

As stated earlier, there are three different methods of tax allocation: (1) the deferred method, (2) the asset-liability method and (3) the net of tax method.

1. The deferred method computes the amount of deferred taxes on the basis of tax rates in effect when the temporary differences originate. No adjustments are made to reflect the changes in tax rates, given that future rates have no relevance. The deferred tax account (debit or credit) is not viewed as an asset or liability, but just as representing the cumulative recognition of the effect of application of the deferred method in past periods. It is the cumulative recognition given to their tax efforts and as such do not represent receivables or payables. The deferred method is considered to be an *income statement–oriented approach* that focuses on the matching of revenues and expenses in the years that the temporary differences originated.

   Among the typical arguments in favor of the deferred method are the following:
   1. The income statement is the most important financial statement, and matching is a critical aspect of the accounting process. Consequently, it is of limited concern that deferred taxes on the balance sheet are not true assets or liabilities in the conceptual sense.
   2. Deferred taxes are the result of historical transactions or events that created the temporary differences. Since accounting reports most economic events on an historical cost basis, deferred taxes should be reported in a similar manner.
   3. Historical income tax rates are verifiable. Reporting deferred taxes based on historical rates increases the reliability of accounting information.[5]

2. The asset/liability method computes the amount of deferred taxes on the basis of the tax rates expected to be in effect when the temporary differences reverse. The enacted tax rates applicable to future years are used to determine the deferred tax asset or liability arising from temporary differences. The deferred tax asset is a receivable for prepaid tax and the deferred tax liability is a liability for tax payable. *It is a balance sheet–oriented approach and is*

the only GAAP requirement. Assuring the typical arguments in favor of the asset/liability method are the following:

1. The balance sheet is an important financial statement. Reporting deferred taxes based upon the enacted future tax rates when the temporary differences reverse increases the predictive value of a corporation's future cash flows, liquidity, and financial flexibility.

2. As discussed earlier, reporting deferred taxes based on the enacted future tax rates is conceptually more sound because the amount represents either the likely future economic sacrifice (future tax payments) or economic benefit (future reduction in taxes).

3. Deferred taxes may be the result of historical transactions but, by definition, they are taxes that are postponed and will be paid (or reduce taxes) in the future at the enacted future tax rates.

4. Estimates are used extensively in accounting. The use of enacted future tax rates for deferred taxes creates information that is, perhaps, more reliable than depreciation based on estimated lives and residual values.[6]

3. The net of tax method does not report any deferred tax account on the balance sheet, set the income taxes payable equal to the income tax expense and report the tax effects of temporary differences as an adjustment to the assets or liabilities and the related revenues and expenses. There are, however, severe limitations to the net of tax display. As stated by Chasteen:

There are several difficulties with net-of-tax display. First, some temporary differences cannot be associated with individual assets or liabilities. Second, if the tax effects of temporary differences were displayed with the individual assets or liabilities, it would be difficult to interpret a company's overall tax situation without significant additional information. Third, the meaning of the resulting balance sheet measure of, for example, building cost less depreciation less deferred less tax liability would be questionable. Finally, a net of tax method reporting is inconsistent with the view that the tax consequences of events recognized currently in the financial statements represent separate assets or liabilities, which is a fundamental concept underlying the asset/liability method.[7]

To illustrate the three methods, let's assume that in 1996 the Valentine Company purchased $200,000 of equipment that has a 10-year useful life and no salvage value. The depreciation expense for financial reporting based on straight-line depreciation method is $20,000. The depreciation for tax purposes is $30,000. The tax rate in 1996 is 40% and is

Exhibit 4.1
Valentine Company: Income Statement

	Deferred Method	Asset-liability Method	Net-of-Tax Method
Income before Depreciation and Income Taxes	$430,000	$430,000	$430,000
Depreciation	20,000	20,000	24,000
Pretax Financial Income	$410,000	$410,000	$406,000
Current Tax Expenses	160,000	160,000	160,000
Deferred Tax Expenses	4,000	5,000	
Total Income Tax Expenses	164,000	165,000	160,000
Net Income	$246,000	$245,00	246,000

enacted to be 50% for future years. The income before depreciation and taxes is $430,000.

For tax purposes the income taxes payable may be imputed as follows:

Income before depreciation and taxes	$430,000
Tax depreciation	30,000
Taxable Income	$400,000
Income taxes payable ($400,000 × 40%)	$160,000

Exhibit 4.1 shows the income statement under each of the three different methods of tax allocation.

A. Under the deferred method, the deferred tax is
   $4,000 [($30,000 − $20,000) × .40]

B. Under the asset-liability method, the deferred tax is
   $5,000 [($30,000 − $20,000) × .50]

C. Under the net-of-tax method the depreciation expense is computed as follows:

Depreciation expense for financial reporting ($200,000/10 years)	$20,000
Tax effect of excess depreciation [($30,000 − $20,000) × .40]	4,000
Depreciation expense under the net-of-tax method	24,000

RECORDING AND REPORTING CURRENT AND DEFERRED TAXES

Procedures for Recording and Reporting Current and Deferred Taxes

The following procedures for the computation and recording of current and deferred taxes are suggested:

1. Classify the existing temporary differences as either "taxable" or "deductible" and identify the nature and amount of each type of operating loss and tax credit carryforward and the expiration dates of all operating loss carryforwards.
2. Measure the deferred tax liability of each taxable temporary differences using the applicable tax rate.
3. Measure the deferred tax assets of each deductible temporary differences using the applicable tax rate; do the same for operating loss carryforwards.
4. Measure the deferred tax assets for each type of tax credit carryforward.
5. Reduce deferred tax assets by a *valuation allowance* if, based on available evidence, it is *more likely than not* that some or all deferred tax assets will not be realized.
6. Measure the income tax obligation using the applicable tax rate to the current taxable income.
7. Report in the income statement the current tax expense, the deferred tax expense and the total income tax expense.
8. Report in the balance sheet the charge in deferred tax liabilities and/or deferred tax assets, and charges in valuation allowance (if any) and classify the amounts as current or noncurrent.

Application of these procedures results in use of three basic entries:

A. The first case involves a situation where the temporary differences are taxable temporary differences existing at the end of the current year resulting in a deferred tax liability that represents the increase in taxes payable in future years. The entry is as follows:

Income Tax Expense	XXX	
Deferred Tax Liability		XXX
Income Taxes Payable		XXX

B. The second case involves a situation where the temporary differences are deductible temporary differences existing at the end of the current year resulting in a deferred tax asset that represents the increase in taxes refundable (or saved).

Income Tax Expense	XXX	
Deferred Tax Asset	XXX	
Income Tax Payable		XXX

C. The last case involves the situation where based on available evidence it is more likely than not that some of the deferred tax will not be realized, requiring the recognition of a valuation allowance as follows:

Income Tax Expense	XXX	
Allowance to Reduce		
Deferred Tax		XXX
Asset to Realizable Value		XXX

In these three cases the amounts are calculated as follows:

1. Income tax expense is allocated to the various components of *earnings* comprehensive income (intraperiod allocation)
2. Income tax payable = taxable income × current tax rate(s)
3. The adjustment to deferred tax liability (asset) is obtained by comparing the year-end deferred tax liability (asset) with the beginning deferred tax liability (asset)
4. The year-end deferred tax liability (asset) is reported as current and noncurrent.
5. The balance sheet shows an expected net realized value of the deferred tax asset after deducting the allowance account from the deferred tax asset account.

Example of a Deferred Tax Liability

To illustrate a deferred tax liability, let's assume that in 1995, the Monti Company had revenues of $360,000 for book purposes and $300,000 for tax purposes. It also had expenses of $160,000 for both financial and tax reporting. The income for 1995 would be as follows:

	Financial Income	Taxable Income
Revenues	$360,000	$300,000
Expenses	160,000	160,000
Pretax Financial Income for 1995	$200,000	
Taxable Income		$140,000
Income Tax Payable for 1995 (assuming a 40% tax rate)		56,000
		$84,000

The end of 1995 asset difference would be:

	GAAP	Tax Reporting
Accounts receivable:	$60,000	-0-

Therefore the $60,000 difference in book value ($60,000 − 0) is a result of temporary difference in revenue that originated in 1995 causing taxable income to be lower than financial income for that year. It is a *taxable temporary difference* because taxable income will be higher than financial income in future years. The deferred tax liability is computed as $60,000 × 40% = $24,000 (the total taxable temporary difference × the enacted future tax rate).

The income tax expense will be as follows:

1. Deferred tax liability at the end of 1995 $24,000

2. Deferred tax liability at the beginning of 1995 -0-

3. Deferred tax expense for 1995 $24,000

4. Current tax expense for 1995 56,000

5. Total Income Tax Expense for 1995 $80,000

The basic entry is as follows:

Income Tax Expense	80,000	
Income Tax Payable		56,000
Deferred Tax Liability		24,000

Now let's assume that the Monti Company expects to receive $20,000 of the receivables in 1997 and $40,000 of the receivables in 1996.

At the end of 1996 the difference between the book basis and the tax basis is $20,000. Therefore the deferred tax liability to be reported at the end of 1996 is $8,000 ($20,000 × 40%). If the current tax expense for 1996 is $90,000, then the total income tax expense for 1996 will be as follows:

1. Deferred tax liability at the end of 1996	$8,000
2. Deferred tax liability at the beginning of 1996	$24,000
3. Deferred tax expense (benefit) for 1996	(16,000)
4. Current tax expense for 1996	90,000
5. Total income tax expense for 1996	$74,000

The basic entry is as follows:

Income Tax Expense	74,000	
Deferred Tax Liability	16,000	
Income Tax Liability		90,000

At the end of 1997 the deferred tax liability is reduced by the remaining $8,000 to bring the account to a zero balance.

Second Example of a Deferred Tax Liability

Let's assume that in 1995 the Arafat Company purchased an asset with a cost of $12,000, a four-year life, no residual value, and a depreciation based on the units-of-output method over 12,000 units (1996: 1,000 units, 1997: 5,000 units, 1998: 4,000 units, 1999: 2,000 units). MACRS using 200% declining balance method over a three-year life is used for tax depreciation. The MACRS depreciation as a percentage of the cost of the asset is shown in Exhibit 4.2. In addition, the Arafat

Exhibit 4.2
MACRS Depreciation as a Percentage of the Cost of the Asset

Year of Life	Tax Life of Asset in Years					
	3	5	7	10	15	20
1	33.33%	20.00%	14.29%	10.00%	5.00%	3.750%
2	44.45	32.00	24.49	18.00	9.50	7.219
3	14.81	19.20	17.49	14.40	8.55	6.677
4	7.41	11.52	12.49	11.52	7.70	6.177
5		11.52	8.93	9.22	6.93	5.713
6		5.76	8.92	7.37	6.23	5.285
7			8.93	6.55	5.90	4.888
8			4.46	6.55	5.90	4.522
9				6.56	5.91	4.462
10				6.55	5.90	4.461
11				3.28	5.91	4.462
12					5.90	4.461
13					5.91	4.462
14					5.90	4.461
15					5.91	4.462
16					2.95	4.461
17						4.462
18						4.461
19						4.462
20						4.461
21						2.231

Company had a taxable income of $15,000 and the 30% tax rate is enacted for years.

First: the depreciation expense for financial reporting is $1,000 [1,000 × ($12,000/12,000)], and depreciation expense for tax purposes using Exhibit 4.2 is $4,000 ($12,000 × 33.33%).

Second: At the end of 1995 the asset has a book value of $11,000 ($12,000 − $1,000) for financial reporting and a book value of $8,000 ($12,000 − $4,000) for tax purposes.

Third: There is a $3,000 ($11,000 − $8,000) taxable temporary difference because future taxable income will be higher than future pretax financial income.

Fourth: The deferred liability is $900 ($3,000 × 30%).

Fifth: The current tax expense for 1995 is $4,500 ($15,000 × 30%).

Sixth: The income tax expense will be as follows:

1. Deferred tax liability at the end of 1995	$900
2. Deferred tax liability at the beginning of 1995	-0-
3. Deferred tax expense for 1995	$900
4. Current tax expense for 1995	4,500
5. Total income tax expense for 1995	$5,400

The basic entry is as follows:

Income Tax Expense	$5,400	
Deferred Tax Liability		900
Income Taxes Payable		4,500

Example of a Deferred Tax Asset

To illustrate a deferred tax asset, let's assume that in 1996 the Gasparetti Company, which provides a two-year warranty on the product it sells, estimated its warranty liability to be $60,000. For financial reporting purposes the company records a warranty liability at the end of the year. For income tax purposes, it deducts the warranty costs only when paid. Therefore the $60,000 warranty liability is a *deductible temporary difference* (deferred tax asset) because in the future the warranty costs deducted for income tax purposes will be greater than the warranty expenses for financial reporting, causing taxable income to be lower than pretax financial income. Let's assume also that at the beginning of the year 1996 the deferred tax asset was $20,000 corresponding to the warranty liability in the balance sheet. The taxable income for 1996 was $80,000. The rate for 1995 and the following years is 40%.

A. At the end of 1996 the asset difference would be:

	Book Basis	**Tax Basis**
Warranty liability	$60,000	-0-

B. The deferred tax asset is computed as $24,000 ($60,000 × 40%)

C. The current tax expense for 1996 is $32,000 ($80,000 × 40%)

D. The total income tax expense for 1996 is as follows:
1. Deferred tax asset at end of 1996 $24,000
2. Deferred tax asset at beginning of 1996   20,000
3. Deferred tax expense (benefit) for 1996 $(4,000)
4. Current tax expense for 1996   32,000
5. Income tax expense (total) for 1996 $28,000

E. The basic entry at the end of 1996 is as follows:

Income Tax Expense	$28,000	
Deferred Tax Asset	4,000	
Income Tax Payable		32,000

F. Assuming the income tax payable for 1997 is $40,000, the total income tax expense is as follows:
1. Deferred tax asset at the end of 1997
(The difference between the book value and the tax basis of the liability is zero) $-0-
2. Deferred tax asset at the beginning of 1997 $4,000
3. Deferred tax expense (benefits) for 1997   4,000
4. Current tax expense for 1997   40,000
5. Total income tax expense for 1997 $44,000

G. The basic entry at the end of 1997 is as follows:

Income Tax Expense	44,000	
Deferred Tax Asset		4,000
Income Tax Payable		40,000

H. The income statement presentation will be as follows:

Revenues	XXX

Expenses	<u>XXX</u>	
Income before Income Taxes	XXX	

Income Tax Expense		
Current	40,000	
Deferred	<u>4,000</u>	<u>44,000</u>
Net Income		XXX

Example of a Deferred Tax Asset and Valuation Allowance

Let's assume that same information as in the previous example involving the Gasparetti Company, and after a careful review of evidence, it is decided at the end of 1996 that it is more likely than not that $10,000 of the deductible temporary difference will not be realized. The Gasparetti Company needs to recognize a valuation allowance of $4,000 ($10,000 × 40%).

The basic entries at the end of 1996 are:

A. Income Tax Expense	28,000	
Deferred Tax Asset	4,000	
Income Tax Payable		32,000

B. Income Tax Expense		
Allowance to Reduce Deferred		
Tax	$4,000	
Asset to Expected		
Realizable Value		$4,000

C. The balance sheet will show the net deferred asset as follows:

Deferred Tax Asset	$24,000
Less: Allowance to Reduce Deferred Tax Asset to Expected Realizable Value	4,000
Deferred Tax Asset (Net)	$20,000

The allowance is to be evaluated at the end of each year and adjusted if necessary.

Example of Permanent and Temporary Differences

To illustrate the case of both permanent and temporary differences, let's assume that the Picur Company reports pretax income of $100,000 for 1995. The following permanent and temporary differences are noted:

1. Permanent difference:
   The Picur Company received an interest revenue of $10,000 on municipal bonds.

2. Taxable temporary difference:
   The Picur Company recognized under accrual accounting a gross profit of $50,000 on installment sales and collected $30,000.

3. Deductible temporary differences:
   The Picur Company received a $21,000 rental revenue received in advance on a three-year contract stipulating a $7,000 rent revenue per year.

In addition, the Picur Company had a deferred tax liability of $4,000 arising from the installment sales temporary difference at the beginning of the year. The income tax rate for 1995 and following years is 40%. Exhibit 4.3 reconciles the pretax financial income to the taxable income in a manner similar to Form 1120 of the IRC.

The basic entry is as follows:

Deferred Tax Asset	5,600	
Income Tax Expense ($33,600		
-- $5,600 + $4,000)	32,000	
Deferred Tax Liability		$4,000
Income Taxes Payable		33,600

where:

A. The deferred tax liability is $4,000, the difference between $8,000, the deferred tax liability for the installment sales at the end of the year ($20,000 × 40%), and $4,000, the deferred tax liability at the beginning of the year.

B. The deferred tax asset is $5,600, the difference between $5,600, the deferred tax asset for the rent revenue temporary difference at the end of the year

Exhibit 4.3
Picur Company: Computation of 1995 Taxable Income

Pretax Financial Income	$200,000
less:	
1. The permanent difference arising from the tax-exempt interest revenue on municipal bonds.	(10,000)
2. The temporary difference of excess of gross profit on installment sales over gross profit over taxes.	($20,000)
Plus The temporary difference of excess new collected in advance over rent revenue	14,000
Taxable Income	$84,000
Current Income Tax ($84,000 x 40%)	$33,600

($14,000 × 40%) and $0, the deferred tax asset for the rent revenue at the beginning of the year.

Changes in Enacted Tax Rates

The enacted changes in tax rates that become effective for future years should be used when determining the tax rate to apply to existing temporary differences. To illustrate the changes in enacted tax rates, let's assume that in 1995 the Camelli Company had a receivable of $12,000 in its balance sheet. The amount is the difference between the $20,000 asset (and revenue) recognized in 1995 for financial reporting and the $8,000 cash collection recognized for tax purposes. The difference is expected to reverse and become a taxable amount of $8,000 in 1996 and $4,000 in 1997. The enacted tax rate is 35%. The current tax expense is $4,000.

A. The deferred tax liability for 1995 is $12,000 × .35 = $4,200

B. The basic entry at the end of 1995 is as follows:

Income Tax Expense	8,200	
Income Tax Payable		4,000
Deferred Tax Liability		4,200

C. The deferred tax expense for 1996 is as follows:
   1. Deferred tax liability at the
      end of 1996 ($4,000 × .35)   1,400
   2. Deferred tax liability at the
      beginning of 1996   4,200
   3. Deferred tax expense
      (benefit) for 1996   (2,800)

D. The basic entry for 1996 is as follows:
   Deferred Tax Liability   2,800
      Income Tax Payable   2,800

E. The remaining balance of $1,400 in deferred tax liability is eliminated in 1997:
   Deferred Tax Liability   1,400
      Income Tax Payable   1,400

Now, let's assume that at the end of 1996 there is a newly enacted tax rate of 40% for 1997. The deferred tax liability has to be adjusted to reach the remaining tax consequences of the temporary difference of $4,000 at the end of 1996. The basic entry at the end of 1996 is as follows:

   Deferred Tax Liability
   [$4,200 − (.40 × $4,000)]   2,600
   Income Tax Expense
   [$2,800 − $2,600]   200
      Income Taxes Payable
      [.35 × $8,000]   2,800

Basically, the following happened:

A. The income tax rate did not change for 1996 so the Income Taxes Payable is $2,800 [.35 × $8,000]

B. The Deferred Tax Liability used to be adjusted from the beginning of 1996 balance of $4,200 to a new desired balance of $1,600 [.40 × $4,000], a difference of $2,600 [$4,200 − $1,600].

C. The tax consequences are now expected to be $8,400 ($8,200 + $200) instead of the $8,200 estimated at the end of 1995. The $200 is an additional income tax expense in 1996.

OPERATING LOSS CARRYBACKS AND CARRYFORWARDS

A firm sometimes faces the situation of a taxable loss where the tax deductible expenses are higher than the taxable revenues. To provide relief to a firm experiencing net operating loss, the Internal Revenue Code (IRC) allows the firm to carry the loss back or carry it forward to offset previous or taxable income. The firm may elect to carry the loss back for three years in a sequential order starting with the earliest of the three years. The technique is known as *operating loss carryback*, that allows an amendment of the income tax returns and lowers the taxable income of the previous three years and the receipt of a refund of income taxes. If there is no sufficient previous taxable income for the three years, the firm carries the loss sequentially forward 15 years to offset future taxable income. The technique is known as *operating loss carryforward*.

The GAAP for this issue, as enunciated in FASB No. 109 call for (a) the recognition of the tax benefit of an operating loss carryback in the period of the loss as a current receivable on the balance sheet and a reduction of the operating loss in the income statement; (b) the recognition of the tax benefit of an operating loss carryforward in the period of the loss as a deferred tax, to be reduced by a valuation allowance if, based on available evidence, it is more likely than not that some or all of the deferred taxes will not be realized.

Example of an Operating Loss Carryback

To illustrate the case of an operating loss carryback, let's assume that in 1996 the Dali Company faces the following results.

Year	Taxable Income (loss)	Tax Rate	Taxes Paid
1993	$50,000	20%	$10,000
1994	50,000	25%	12,500
1995	100,000	30%	30,000
1996	(250,000)	40%	

Because the company faces an operating loss of ($250,000) in 1996, it may elect to carry back the loss and be entitled to a tax refund of $52,500 as illustrated below.

Year	Pretax Financial Income and Taxable Income Offset by Carryback	Tax Rate	Tax Refund
1993	$50,000	20%	$10,000
1994	50,000	25%	12,500
1995	100,000	30%	30,000
	$200,000		$52,500

The tax benefit of the loss carryback is $52,500. The basic entry at the end of 1996 is as follows:

Income Tax Refund Receivable	52,500	
Income Tax Benefit from		
Operating Loss Carryback		52,500

The $52,500 receivable is shown in the balance sheet as a current asset until the receipt of the refund from the IRS. The 1996 income statement will disclose the income tax benefit as follows:

Pretax Operating Loss		($250,000)
Loss: Income Tax Benefit for	52,500	
Operating Loss Carryback		($197,500)

Notice that ($250,000) net operating loss for 1995 is higher than the $200,000 taxable income of 1993–1995, resulting in a remaining $50,000 operating loss that is to be carried forward.

Example of an Operating Loss Carryforward and No Valuation Allowance

Returning to the previous example on the Dali Company, the remaining $50,000 operating loss is to be carried forward resulting in a deferred tax of $20,000 ($50,000 × 40%). The basic entries in 1996 should be:

a. Income Tax Refund		
Receivable	52,500	
Income Tax Benefit from		
Operating Loss Carryback		52,500

This entry is similar to the previous entry, intended to recognize the operating loss carryback to three previous years.

b. Deferred Tax Asset	20,000	
Income Tax Benefit from		
Operating Loss		
Carryforward		20,000

Therefore the financial statements include the following new information:

a. The balance sheet will include an income tax refundable receivable of $52,500 as a current asset a deferred tax asset of $20,000.

b. The 1995 income statement will disclose the income tax benefits as follows.

Pretax Operating loss	$(250,000)
Income Tax Benefit	
a. Benefit from Operating Loss Carryback	52,500
b. Benefit from Operating Loss Carryforward	20,000
	($177,500)

Let's now assume that in 1997 the Dali Company has a taxable income of $300,000 and the tax rate is still 40%. Given the benefits of the operating loss carryforward recognized in 1996, the income tax payable for 1997 would be as follows:

1. Taxable Income Prior to the Loss Carryforward	$300,000
2. Less Loss Carryforward	50,000
3. Taxable Income	$250,000
4. Income Taxes Payable for 1996 (at 40%)	100,000

Accordingly, the basic entry at the end of 1997 would be as follows:

Income Tax Expense	120,000	
Deferred Tax Asset		20,000
Income Taxes Payable		100,000

The lower portion of the 1997 income statement is as follows:

| Pretax Operating Income | $300,000 |

Income Tax Expense		
Current	100,000	
Deferred	20,000	120,000
Net Income		180,000

Example of an Operating Loss Carryforward and Valuation Allowance

Returning again to the Dali Company, let's assume that in 1996 there is insufficient positive evidence of future taxable income. There is a need for a valuation allowance to reduce the deferred asset. Therefore, the basic entries at the end of 1996 are as follows:

a. Income Tax Refund Receivable	52,500	
Income Tax Benefit from Operating Loss Carryback		52,500
b. Deferred Tax Asset	20,000	
Income Tax Benefit Operating Loss Carryforward		20,000
c. Income Tax Benefit from Operating Loss Carryforward	20,000	
Allowance to Reduce Deferred Tax Asset to Expected Realizable Value		20,000

Again, assuming that in 1997 the Dali Company experiences a taxable income of $300,000 and the tax rate is still 40%, the following entries will be made.

a. Income Tax Expense	120,000	
Deferred Tax Asset		20,000
Income Taxes Payable		100,000
b. Allowance to Reduce Deferred Tax Asset to Expected Realizable Value	20,000	

Income Tax Benefit from Operating Loss Carryforwards (Income Tax Expenses)		20,000

The two entries could be combined as follows:

Income Tax Expense	100,000	
Allowance to Reduce Tax Asset to Expected Realizable Value	20,000	
Deferred Tax Asset		20,000
Income Taxes Payable		100,000

INTRAPERIOD INCOME TAX ALLOCATION

Intraperiod income tax allocation involves the allocation of a firm's total income tax expense for a period (computed using the deferred tax procedures) to all the elements of the income statements and balance sheets that it affects. The items include:

1. Income from continuing operations.
2. Gains and losses from discontinued operations.
3. Extraordinary gains and losses.
4. Cumulative effects of changes in accounting principles reported in the income statement.
5. Stockholders' equity items.

The types of items included in stockholders' equity items are as follows:

1. Prior period adjustments to beginning retained earnings.
2. Gains and losses from transactions reported in the comprehensive income as defined in the conceptual framework but not in the net income.
3. Different reporting of costs for tax and book income purposes for stock option plans under Opinion No. 25.
4. Changes in paid-in-capital.
5. Dividend payments changed to retained earnings for shares of stock related to an ESOP.

6. Temporary differences that are deductible and carryforwards on the date an entity had a quasi-reorganization.

7. Increase in the tax basis of assets where a tax benefit was recognized for assets acquired in a taxable involving-of-interest business combination.

8. Foreign currency translation adjustments.

9. Additional pension liability reported in stockholders' equity.

The procedure for intraperiod tax allocation is described as follows:

Income tax expenses or tax benefit computed for the accounting period is applied to the items on the income statement and balance sheet that are required to be reported net of tax using an incremental approach. First, income tax expense or tax benefit (tax expense/benefit) computed on income from continuing operations, assuming no other income or losses, is allocated to income from continuing operations. This amount is adjusted for the tax impact of (1) changes in judgement about deferred tax asset realization, (2) tax law or rate changes, (3) tax status changes, and (4) dividends to stockholders that are tax deductible (Paragraph 35). Second, the tax expense/benefit on total income is determined, and the excess of the tax expense/benefit on total income less the tax expense/benefit on income from continuing operations is the total incremental tax expense/benefit. The incremental tax expense/benefit is allocated to all items requiring intraperiod tax allocations, except income continuing operations.[8]

If the total incremental tax does not equal the sum of the incremental tax effects of two or more items, the allocation process requires a formula basis. A formula basis is included in the following four-step procedure.

The intraperiod tax allocation rests in the following four steps.

1. The tax benefit of the total net loss items, excluding loss from continuing operations, is determined.

2. The tax benefit computed above is allocated ratably to each loss item.

3. The tax impact of all gains and losses, excluding income from continuing operations is determined.

4. The difference between the tax benefit of the total net loss items and the tax impact of all gains and losses is allocated in each gain category.[9]

To illustrate, assume the Preschel Company reports the following information.

First Example of Intraperiod Tax Allocation

A. The income, gains and losses of the Preschel Company in 1995 is as follows:

Income from continuing operations	$43,000
Loss from segment disposition	(23,000)
Extraordinary gain—Gain from expropriation of assets	45,000
Cumulative effect of a change in accounting principle	(7,000)
Total	$58,000

B. The Preschel Company had the following tax rates for 1995.

$0 – $50,000	15%
$50,000 – $75,000	25%
over $75,000	34%
$100,000–$335,000	5% additional tax

The first step is to compute the total incremental tax as follows:

1. Tax on income from continuing operations.
   $43,000 × 15%   =$6,450

2. Tax on total income.
a. $50,000 × 15%	= $7500	
b. 8,000 × 95%	=2000	
c. Total	$9,500	9,500

3. Total Incremental Tax   3,050

The second step is to complete the incremental tax for all loss categories. It is shown in Exhibit 4.4.

The third step is the allocation of incremental tax to gains and losses. It is shown in Exhibit 4.5.

The fourth step is the presentation of the allocation to each income, gain and loss item. It is shown in Exhibit 4.6.

The final step is the preparation of the income statement as shown in Exhibit 4.7.

Second Example of Intraperiod Tax Allocation

To illustrate the second example of intraperiod tax allocation, assume the Tucker Company reports the following items of pretax financial (and taxable) income for 1997:

Exhibit 4.4
Allocation of Incremental Tax to Gains and Losses

Computation of Percentages for Allocations:

Incremental tax on segment dispositon	$6890	
Incremental tax on accounting change	1750	
Total incremental tax on segment disposition	$8640	
Incremental tax on segment disposition	$6890	
		= 79.74%
Total incremental tax on losses computed separately	8,640	
Incremental tax on accounting change	1,750	
		=20.25%
Total incremental tax on losses computed seperately	8,640	

Allocation of Incremental Tax to Losses:

	Segment Disposition	Accounting Change	Total
Incremental tax on losses computed together	$8670	$8670	
Percentages	79.74%	20.25%	
Allocation of incremental tax to losses	$6914	$1756	$8670

Allocation of Incremental Tax to Gains:

Total incremental tax for losses computed together	$8670
Total incremental tax	3050
Incremental tax allocated to extraordinary item	$11720

Revenues	190,000	
Expenses	100,000	
Income from continuing operations		$90,000
Gain on disposal of discontinued segment		20,000
Loss from operations on discontinued segment		(7,000)
Extraordinary loss on bond redemption		(12,000)
Cumulative effect of a change in accounting principle		
(accelerated depreciation to straight line)		17,000

Exhibit 4.5
Incremental Tax for All Loss Categories

	Segment Disposition and Accounting Change	Segment Disposition	Accounting Change
Total income...	$58,000	$58,000	$58,000
Losses from loss categories.......................	30,000	25,000	7,000
Total income without each loss category...	$88,000	$81,000	$65,000
Income tax without losses (from below)..	$18,170	$15,790	$11,250
Total tax (from above)...............................	(9500)	(9500)	(9500)
Incremental tax expense...........................	$ 8670	$ 6290	$ 1750

Computation of Tax on Loss Categories:
$50,000 x 15%..	$7,500
25,000 x 25%..	6,250
13,000 x 34%..	4,420
88,000	$18,170

$50,000 x 15%..	$7,500
25,000 x 25%..	6,250
13,000 x 34%..	2,040
81,000	$15,790

$50,000 x 15%..	$7,500
15,000 x 25%..	3,750
$65,000	$11,250

Prior period adjustment (error in computing bad debt expense in 1996)	(9,000)
Amount subject to income taxes	$99,000

The company is taxed at 15% on the first $50,000 of income and 20% on income exceeding $50,000. The allocation of income tax expense is illustrated in Exhibit 4.8. The Tucker Company income statement for 1997 as well as the statement of retained earnings are illustrated in Exhibit 4.9.

The 1997 entry to record the intraperiod tax allocation of the Tucker Company is as follows:

Exhibit 4.6

Presentation of Allocation to Each Income, Gain and Loss Item

	Income/ (Loss)	(Expense)/ Benefit	Amounts After Tax
Income from continuing operations	$43,000	$(6450)	$36,550
Segment disposition (16086)	(23,000)	6914	
Extraordinary items	45,000	(11720)	33280
Accounting items	(7,000)	1756	(5244)
Total Income	$58000	$ 9500	$48500

Exhibit 4.7

Preschel Company: Partial Income Statement for the Year Ended December 31, 1995

Income from continuing operations before tax	$43,000
Income Tax Expense	6,450
Income from continuing operations	$36,550
Segment disposition, net of tax $6,914	(16,086)
Extraordinary Items:	
Gain from expropriation of assets, net tax of $11,720	33,280
Cumulative effect of a change in accounting principle, net of tax $1,756	(5,244)
Net Income	$48,500

Income Tax Expense	15,500	
Gain on Disposal of Segment	3,000	
Cumulative Effect of Change in Account Principle	2,550	
Loss from Operations of Discontinued Segment		1,050
Extraordinary Loss on Bond Redemption		1,800
Retained Earnings (Prior Period Adjustments)		1,350
Income Taxes Payable		16,850

Exhibit 4.8
Tucker Company: Schedule of Income Tax Expense for 1997

Items (Pretax)	Pretax x Tax Amount Rate	=	Income Tax Expense (Credit)
Income from continuing operations	$50,000 x 0.15	=	$7500
	40,000 x 0.20	=	8000
Gain on disposal of discontinued segment	20,000 x 0.15	=	3000
Loss from operations on discounted segment	(7,000 x 0.15)	=	(1050)
Extraordinary loss on bond redemption	(12,000 x 0.15)	=	(1800)
Cumulative effect of a change in accounting principle	17,000 x 0.15	=	2550
Prior period adjustment	(9,000 x 0.15)	=	(1350)
Total income tax expense			$16,850

Exhibit 4.9
Tucker Company: Income Statement for the Year 1997

Revenues		$190,000
Expenses		90,000
Pretax Income from Continuity Operations		90,000
Income tax expense		15,500
Income from continuing operations		74,500
Results of discontinued operations		
Gain on disposal of discontinued segment (net of $3000 income tax)	$17,000	
Loss from operations of discontinued segment (net of $1050 income tax credit)	(5,950)	11,050
Income before extraordinary loss		$85,550
Extraordinary loss or bond redemption (net of $1800 income tax credit)		(10,200)
Cumulative effect of a change in accounting principle (net of $2550 income taxes)		14,450
Net income		$87,800

Statement of Retained Earnings for the Year 1997

Retained Earnings, Jan.1,1997	207,650
loss: Prior period adjustment, understatement of 1996 paid debt expense (net of $1350 income tax credit)	(7,650)
Adjustment Retained Earnings, Jan. 1, 1997	200,000
Add: Net Income	89,900
	289,900
less Cash Dividends	(30,000)
Retained Earnings, Dec. 31, 1997.	259,900

NOTES

1. "Accounting for Income Taxes," *FASB Statement of Financial Accounting Standards No. 109* (Stamford, Conn.: FASB, 1992).

2. With the exception of (a) long-term contracts using percentage of completion for tax and modified method for tax and (b) organizational costs expensed for financial accounting and deferred for tax, all the other temporary differences between financial accounting income and tax income cause differences between book and tax basis of assets and liabilities. For the two exceptions, the revenue or expense is reported on tax balance sheet but not on financial accounting balance sheet.

3. "Accounting for Income Taxes," par. 6 and 8.

4. Loren A. Nikolai and John D. Bazely, *Intermediate Accounting*, 6th ed. (Cincinnati, Ohio: South-Western Publishing Co., 1994), p. 818.

5. Ibid., p. 850.

6. Ibid., p. 849.

7. Ianny G. Chasteen, Richard E. Flaherty, and Melvin C. O'Connor, *Intermediate Accounting*, 5th ed. (New York: McGraw-Hill, 1995), p. 855.

8. Bill D. Jarnagin, *Financial Accounting Standards: Explanation and Analysis*, 18th ed.—1996 (Chicago: CCH Incorporated, 1996), p. 405.

9. Ibid.

5

Accounting for Pensions

INTRODUCTION

Security after retirement is a major concern of every U.S. citizen. In response, Congress passed in 1935 the Federal Insurance Contribution Act (also called Social Security) requiring most employees and employers to contribute to a federal retirement program. Because it was not enough, firms have also adopted private pension plans. A pension plan is an arrangement between a firm and its employees whereby the firm agrees to provide retired employees with benefits, such as periodic payments or lump-sum distributions, in return for the services they provided during their employment. The growing size and importance of these pension plans encouraged Congress to pass the Employee Retirement Income Security Act of 1974 (ERISA), also referred to as the Pension Reform Act of 1974, with the objective of protecting employees' pension rights by legislating various pension requirements, including minimum funding, participation and vesting. One interesting feature of ERISA is the creation of the Pension Benefit Guaranty Corporation (PBGC) to administer terminated plans and impose basis on employers' assets for unfunded pension liabilities. To avoid firms' continuing to shift their responsibilities to the federal government, Congress enacted the Multiemployer Pension Plan Amendments Act of 1980, which allows PBGC to provide coverage only for insolvent plans and not unfunded plans, and improves important obligations for a part of a plan's unfunded vested benefits on firms withdrawing from multiemployer plans. To help in the administration and accounting of these pension plans, the FASB issued, in December 1985, FASB Statement No 87, "Employers' Accounting for Pensions,"[1] and in December 1990 FASB Statement No. 106, "Employers' Accounting for Postretirement Benefits other than Pensions."[2]

PENSION PLAN TERMINOLOGY

A pension plan can be either a *defined contribution plan* or a *defined benefit plan*. The defined contribution plan implies that the employer is contributing to a pension trust a given amount each year based on a formula and the benefits are defined by the contributions and the returns from the investments of the contributions. Accounting for defined contribution plan is simple with pension annual expense limited to the required contribution to the pension trust. If the amount given by the firm is less than the required contribution, a liability is created. If the amount is higher than the required contribution, an asset is reported. In addition, the firm is required to disclose a description of the plan that includes employee groups covered, when the contributions were determined and factors affecting comparability from year to year.

The defined benefit plan implies that the benefits to be received by the employees after retirement or the method of determining them are explicitly stated. The amounts needed to fund the pension plan are determined by actuaries on the basis of actuarial funding methods. The plan is considered noncontributory if the firm or employer is solely responsible for the total contribution of a trust or funding agency. In general, companies insure that their plans meet the IRC qualifications, designing them as qualified pension plans to insure that (a) the employer contributions are deductible for income tax purposes and (b) the pension fund earnings from pension fund assets are tax free. What appears from the above description is the need for a distinct accounting for the pension by the employer, and accounting for the pension fund.[3] This chapter is concerned strictly with accounting for pension by the employer.

PENSION LIABILITIES

The first important question relates to the amount of the pension obligation or liability. Three alternative measures of pension liability exist:

1. *The vested benefits obligation* as the present value of estimated vested benefits using current salary levels where vested benefits are those for which the

employee's right to receive a present or future pension is no longer contingent on remaining in the service of the employer.

2. *The accumulated benefit obligation* (ABO) as the present value of estimated benefits for vested and nonvested employees using current salaries.

3. *The projected benefit obligation* (PBO) as the present value of estimated benefits for vested and nonvested employees at future salaries. PBO is the measure of liability adopted by GAAP, although ABO is also used in certain cases. It is computed as follows:

PBO = Total Benefits Earned × Present Value of Annuity for Period of Retirement × Present Value of $1 for Remaining Period of Employment

PENSION EXPENSE

The second important question relates to the computation of pension expense using an accrual approach. It includes five components: service cost, interest on the liability, actual return on plan assets, amortization of unrecognized prior service cost and gain or loss. They are explicated next.

1. *Service Cost*: The service cost is the actuarial present value of the benefits attributed by the pension benefit formula to services rendered by employees during the period. It is an increase in pension benefits payable (PBO) for services rendered during the period.

2. *Interest Cost or Interest on the Liability*: The interest cost is the increase in the projected benefit obligation due to the passage of time, using a discount rate provided by the actuary and called the *settlement rate*.

3. *Actual Return on Plan Assets*: The actual return on plan assets is the difference between the fair value of the plan assets at the end of the period and the fair value at the beginning of the period, adjusted for contributions by the firm and payments of benefits to retired employees during the period. The plan assets—usually stocks, bonds and other investments—that have been segregated and restricted (usually in a trust) to provide benefits, generate either a positive return that is subtracted in the computation of pension expense, or a negative return that is added to the computation of pension expense.

4. *Amortization of Unrecognized Prior Service Cost*: Retroactive benefits are often granted in plan amendment that are attributed by the pension benefit formula to employee services rendered in periods prior to the amendment. The cost of retroactive benefit granted in a plan amendment is referred to as prior services cost. Prior services cost is not recognized in the financial state-

ments in total in the period granted. However, this unrecognized prior service cost is amortized to pension expense in the future, specifically to the remaining service life of the affected employees. The amortization of unrecognized prior service cost is added in the computation of pension expense.

5. *Gain or Loss*: Changes in the value of either the projected benefit obligation because of a change in actuarial assumption or in the plan assets because of experience different from that assumed result in gains or losses are included in the computation of the pension expense. This gain or loss is the sum of: (a) the difference between the actual return on plan assets and the expected return on plan assets, and (b) the amortization of unrecognized net gain or loss from previous periods if at the beginning of the years the cumulative unrecognized net gain or loss from previous periods exceeds 10% of the greater of the actual projected benefit (PBO) or the fair value of the plan assets.

As a result, the gain and the loss component of pension expense consists of two of the following four items:

1. An increase to pension expense for the excess of actual return on plan assets minus expected return on plan assets, or

2. A decrease to pension expense for the excess of expected return on plan assets minus actual return on plan assets, and

3. An increase to pension for the amortization of any unrecognized net loss from previous periods, or

4. A decrease to pension expense for the amortization of any unrecognized gains from previous periods.

PENSION LIABILITIES AND ASSETS

As discussed above, pension expense is defined by GAAP and FASB Statement No. 87, while funding is defined by the rules of ERISA. Therefore, two situations may occur:

1. If pension expense is greater than the amount funded to date, a liability, *prepaid/accrued pension costs* is recognized on the balance sheet.

2. If pension expense is lower than the amount funded to date, an asset, *prepaid/ accrued pension costs* is recognized on the balance sheet.

Notice that from the above situation the FASB has opted not to capitalize as a liability or asset the difference between the projected benefit obligation and the fair value of assets. As a compromise the board opted for the immediate recognition of a *minimum liability* when the accumulated benefit obligation (ABO) exceeds the fair value of plan asset. If a liability for accrued pension cost has already been recognized, an *Additional Pension Liability* has to be reported on the balance sheet and computed as follows:

Additional Pension Liability = Accumulated Benefit Obligation − Fair Value of Plan Assets − Prepaid/Accrued Pension Cost (Credit Balance) + Prepaid/ Accrued Pension Cost (Debit Balance)

The additional pension liability is recognized by a debit to an *Intangible Asset—Deferred Pension Cost* and a credit to Additional Pension Liability. However, if the additional liability exceeds the amount of unrecognized prior service cost, the debit should be to *Excess of Additional Pension Liability over Unrecognized Prior Service Cost* which is to be reported as a contra-account in the stockholders' equity section.

PENSION ACCOUNTING

General Procedures

It appears from the previous discussion the main possible entries for pension accounting are:

a. the recognition of pension expense as follows:

Pension Expense	XXXX	
Cash		XXXX
Prepaid/Accrued Pension Cost		XXXX

or

Pension Expense	XXXX	
Prepaid/Accrued Pension Cost	XXXX	
Cash		XXXX

b. the recognition of additional pension liability as follows:

Intangible Asset-Deferred Pension Cost	XXXX	
Additional Pension Liability		XXXX

or

Excess of Additional Pension Liability over

Unrecognized Prior Services
Cost   XXXX
   Additional Pension Liability   XXXX

Therefore the balance sheet will include the following accounts:

Assets:	Liabilities:
1. Prepaid / Accrued Pension Cost	1. Prepaid / Accrued Pension Cost
(Debit Balance)	(Credit Balance)
Intangible Asset:	2. Additional Pension Liability
2. Deferred Pension Cost	Stockholders' Equity:
	1. Excess of Additional Pension Liability over Unrecognized Prior Service Cost (Contra Account)

In addition, FASB Statement No. 87 requires a schedule reconciling the funded status of the plan with amounts reported on the firm's balance sheet, showing separately.

1. The fair value of plan assets.
2. The projected benefit obligation identifying the accumulated benefits obligation and the vested benefit obligation.
3. The amount of unrecognized prior service cost.
4. The amount of unrecognized gain or loss.

Given the above requirements, a pension worksheet, recommended by Miller,[4] can accommodate the general journal entries required for balance sheet accounts and the memo record entries required for off-balance sheet disclosures. The format of the pension worksheet is as follows:

Pension Worksheet										
Items	General Journal Entries						Memo Record Entries			
	1	2	3	4	5	6	1	2	3	4

The general journal entries are in:

Column 1: for annual pension expense

Column 2: for cash

Column 3: for prepaid/accrued cost

Column 4: for additional liability

Column 5: for pension intangible

Column 6: for the contra-equity account

The memo entries are in:

Column 1: for projected benefit obligation

Column 2: for plan assets

Column 3: for unrecognized prior services cost

Column 4: for unrecognized net gain or loss

This pension worksheet will be used next to illustrate the entries in each of the columns.

Service Cost

The service cost is computed using the benefit/years-of-service method by focusing on future compensation levels in the measurement of the present obligation and periodic pension expense in the plan benefit formula included in them. The service cost is therefore the actuarial present value of benefits attributed by the pension benefit formula to employee service during the period. It is equal to:

Service Cost = Present Value of Future Pension Benefit Earned by Employees in Current Period = Annual Benefits Earned × Present Value of Annuity for Period of Retirement × Present Value of $1 for Remaining Period of Employment

To illustrate, let's assume that the Valentine Company started in January 1996 accounting for a defined pension plan. Some of the facts applying to this plan are as follows:

Plan assets, Jan 1, 1996 are: $200,000

Projected benefit obligation, Jan 1, 1996 is: $200,000

Annual service cost for 1996 is: $18,000

Annual contributions (funding) are: $106,000

Benefits paid to retirees in 1996 are: $198,000

The above data are entered in the worksheet illustrated in Exhibit 5.1. First, the beginning balances of both plan assets and projected benefit obligation of $200,000 are entered in the appropriate memo records columns. Second, the service cost is recorded in entry (1a) as an increase or debit to annual pension expense and an increase or credit to projected benefit obligation. Third, the benefits paid are recorded in entry (1b) as a credit to cash and a debit to plan assets. Finally, the annual contribution is recorded in entry (1c) as a debit to projected benefit obligation and a credit to plan asset.

Interest Cost

Interest cost is basically the increase in the projected benefit obligation as a result of the passage of time, using the rate at which pension benefits could be effectively settled or settlement rate. The following formula will be used:

$$IC = APBOB \times ASR$$

where

IC   = Interest cost component of pension expense
APBOB = Actual projected benefit obligation at the beginning of the accounting period
ASR   = Assumed settlement rate

To illustrate, let's return to the Valentine Company example and assume that the settlement rate for 1996 is 10%. In the worksheet illustrated in Exhibit 5.1, entry (2) records the interest cost of $20,000 (10% × $200,000) as a debit or increase for the annual pension expense and a credit or increase for projected benefit obligation.

Actual Return on Plan Assets

The actual return on plan assets is the increase in pension funds from the return on stocks, bonds and other investments as well as the unreal-

Exhibit 5.1
Valentine Company: 1996 Pension Worksheet

	General Journal Entries						Memo Entries			
	Annual Pension Expense	Cash	Prepaid / Accrued Cost	Additional Liability	Pension Intangible	Contra Equity	Projected Benefit Obligation	Plan Assets	Unrecognized Prior Service Cost	Unrecognized Net Gain or Loss
Balance Jan 1, 1996							$200,000 Cr	$200,000 Dr		
1a. Service Cost	$18,000 Dr						$18,000 Cr			
1b. Benefits							$198,000 Dr	$198,000 Cr		
1c. Contributions		$106,000 Cr						$106,000 Dr		
2. Interest Cost	$20,000 Dr						$20,000 Cr			
3. Actual Return	$20,000 Cr							$20,000 Dr		
4. Prior Service Cost (PSC)							$180,000 Cr		$180,000 Dr	
5. Amortization of PSC	$102,000 Dr								$102,000 Cr	
6. Unexpected Loss	$4,000 Cr									$4,000 Dr
7. Liability Increase							$30,000 Cr			$30,000 Dr
8. Minimum Liability Adj.				$88,000 Cr	$78,000 Dr	$10,000 Dr				
Journal Entry for 1997	$116,000 Dr	$106,000 Cr	$10,000 Cr							
Balance Dec 31, 1996			$10,000 Cr	$88,000 Cr	$78,000 Dr	$10,000 Dr	$250,000 Cr	$128,000 Dr	$78,000 Dr	$34,000 Dr

ized changes in the fair market value of the plan assets. It is computed as follows:

$$ARPA = (FVPAE - C + B) - FVPAB$$

where

ARPA = Actual return on plan assets.
FVPAE = Fair value of plan assets at the end of the period
C = Contributions to plan during the period
B = Benefits paid during the period
FVPAB = Fair value of plan assets at the beginning of the period

To illustrate, let's assume that the actual return on plan assets in 1996 for the Valentine Company is $20,000. Entry (3) in Exhibit 5.1 records the actual return as a credit or decrease in annual pension expense and a debit or increase in plan assets.

Amortization of Unrecognized Prior Service Cost

As discussed earlier, an amendment to the plan may grant retroactive benefits to employee services rendered in periods prior to the amendment. The unrecognized prior service cost is to be recognized as an off-balance-sheet account. These retroactive benefits are to be recognized as pension expense only during the remaining service life of the covered active employees. Therefore two entries are necessary: (1) An entry to recognize in the memo record the increase in the projected benefit obligation and the unrecognized prior service cost at the date of the amendment; (2) an entry to recognize in the journal, as an increase in pension expense and a decrease in unrecognized prior service cost, the amortization of unrecognized prior service cost. The amortization method favored by the FASB is the *years-of-service* amortization method which is similar to the units-of-production computation.

The years-of-service amortization method consists of: (1) Determining the total number of service years in the remaining service life of the covered active employees, (2) obtaining the cost per service year by dividing the unrecognized prior service cost by the total number of service years, and (3) computing the annual amortization charge by multiplying the cost per service year by the number of service years used per year.

To illustrate, let's return to the Valentine Company and assume that the pension plan recognized a $180,000 prior service cost to its employees, covering 340 employees. The expected years of retirements are as follows:

Group	Number of Employees	Expected Retirement at End of Year
1	120	1996
2	180	1997
3	40	1998
Total	340	

The service-years per year and the total service-years are as follows:

Year	Group 1	Group 2	Group 3	Total
1996	120	180	40	340
1997		180	40	220
1998			40	40
Total	120	360	120	600

The cost per service year is therefore $300 ($180,000/600). Finally, the amortization charges are as follows:

Year	Total Service—Years	Cost per Service—Year	Amortization Charge
1996	340	$300	$102,000
1997	220	$300	66,000
1998	40	$300	12,000
Total	600		$180,000

Two entries are included in Exhibit 5.1. Entry (4) records the prior services cost (PSC) of $180,000 as a credit to projected benefit obligations and a debit to unrecognized prior services cost. Entry (5) records the amortization charge of $102,000 as debit to annual pension expense and a credit to unrecognized prior services cost.

Gain or Loss

The gain or loss is the result of the difference between expected rates of return and actual return on both the projected benefit obligation and plan assets. These are generally referred to as actuarial gains and losses. They are of three kinds:

a. Unexpected gain or loss on plan assets, also called asset gains and losses
b. Liability gains and losses
c. Gain or loss subject to amortization

They are examined next.

Asset Gains or Losses

Actuaries use an expected rate of return to compute an expected return on plan assets to be used for the determination of the funding pattern. As a result, a difference may arise between actual and anticipated return on plan assets. Any gain is credited to unrecognized net gain or loss and debited to pension expense. Any loss is debited to unrecognized net gain or loss and credited to pension expense.

Liability Gains or Losses

Actuaries may revise the assumptions used to compute the amount of projected benefit obligation. These unexpected changes in the projected benefit obligation are the liability gains or losses. They are only recognized as an increase or decrease in both the projected benefits obligation and the unrecognized gain or loss memo accounts.

Amortized Net Gain or Loss

To control and limit the growth of the unrecognized gain or loss memo account, the FASB developed a corridor approach for the amortization of the accumulated unrecognized gain or loss when it becomes too large, that is to say, when it exceeds 10% of the larger of the beginning balances of projected benefit obligation or the market value of the plan assets. The amortized net gain or loss is included in the pension expense only if, at the beginning of the year, the unrecognized net gain or loss exceeds the corridor. The amortization charge is computed by dividing the excess gain or loss by the average service years remaining for all participants who are active and anticipate receiving pension plan benefits. To illustrate, let's assume these examples of the Riahi Company, where the average remaining service life of all active employees is six years, has the following data:

Year	Projected Benefit Obligation (a)	Plan Assets (a)	Corridor (b)	Unrecognized Net Loss (a)	Minimum Amortization of Loss (for current year)
1996	$3,100,000	$3,500,000	$350,000	$----0----	$----0----
1997	$3,600,000	$3,900,000	$390,000	$690,000	$50,000 (c)
1998	$3,800,000	$3,600,000	$380,000	$800,000	$176,666 (d)

(a) Values at the beginning of the period
(b) 10% of the greater of projected benefit obligation or market value of plan assets
(c) ($690,000 − $390,000) / 6 = $50,000
(d) ($690,000−50,000+800,000−380,000) / 6 = $176,999

Therefore the pension expense in 1996 should be increased by $50,000.

Accounting for Gain or Loss

Let's return to the Valentine Company example and assume that: (a) the expected rate of return is 12%, and (b) change in actuarial assumptions led to a new estimate of the end-of-the year obligation of $250,000.

Two entries are made to Exhibit 5.1. First entry (6) records the $4,000 unexpected loss [$20,000 − ($200,000 × 12%)] as a credit to annual pension expense and a debit to unrecognized gain or loss. Second entry (7) records the liability increase of $30,000 [$250,000 − ($200,000 + $18,000 + $20,000 + $180,000 − $198,000)] as a credit to projected benefit obligation and a debit to unrecognized net gain or loss.

MINIMUM LIABILITY

To illustrate the minimum liability entries, let's assume that the Valentine Company estimates the minimum liabilities as shown in Exhibit

Exhibit 5.2
Minimum Liability Computation, December 31, 1996

Accumulated Benefit Obligation	$188,000
Plan Assets at Fair Value	$100,000
Unfunded Accumulated Benefit Obligation	($88,000)
(Minimum Liability)	
Accrued Pension Cost	$----0----
Additional Liability	($88,000)
Unrecognized Prior Service Cost	$78,000
Contra Equity Charge	$10,000

5.2. Therefore entry (8) in Exhibit 5.1 records $58,000 as additional liability, $4,000 as a contra-equity and $54,000 as pension intangible.

FINAL JOURNAL ENTRIES

The entries on December 31, 1997 are:

1st Entry:

Pension Expense	$116,000	
Cash		$106,000
Prepaid/Accrued Pension Cost		$10,000

2nd Entry:

Intangible Asset—Deferred Pension Cost	$78,000	
Excess of Additional Pension Liability over Unrecognized Prior Service Cost	$10,000	
Additional Pension Liability		$88,000

NOTES

1. "Employers' Accounting for Pensions," *FASB Statement of Financial Accounting Standards No. 87* (Stamford, Conn.: FASB, 1985).

2. "Employers' Accounting for Postretirement Benefits Other Than Pensions," *FASB Statement of Financial Accounting Standards No. 106* (Stamford, Conn.: FASB, 1990).

3. The accounting and reporting treatment for employee benefit plans is covered in "Accounting and Reporting by Defined Benefit Plans," *FASB Statement of Financial Accounting Standards No. 35* (Stamford, Conn.: FASB, 1979).

4. Paul B. W. Miller, "The New Pension Accounting (Part 2)," *Journal of Accounting* (February 1987), pp. 86–94.

6

Accounting for Leases

INTRODUCTION

Leasing is quickly becoming one of the most popular ways of financing fixed asset acquisitions, producing funds for about a third of the external capital equipment purchased in the United States. As defined in FASB Statement No. 13 (amended and interpreted through January 1990), a lease is an agreement conveying the right to use property, plant, or equipment (land or depreciable assets or both) usually for a stated period of time.[1] The lessor is the owner giving up the right to use the property, plant and equipment and the lessee is the one acquiring the right. Up to the 1960s, firms had the option of reporting the lease information in the notes or disclosing nothing. Then other options included either capitalizing the lease if the lease conveys some ownership rights and privileges or expensing the lease payment if the lease does not convey these rights and privileges. The capitalizing proposals included various views such as (1) capitalize those leases similar to installment purchases, (2) capitalize all long-term leases[2] and capitalize firm leases when the penalty for nonperformance is substantial.[3] The FASB voted for the capitalization approach when the lease transfers substantially all the risks and benefits of the ownership representing in substance a purchase by the lessee and a sale by the lessor, the capitalization applying to noncancellable leases. The capitalization of the present value of future rental payments dictates that the lessee recognizes an asset (leased equipment) and a liability (lease obligation), and the lessor recognizes a receivable

(Net Lease Receivable) and a credit to equipment. Three entries that are required, depending on the complexity of the situation, are treated in the remainder of this chapter.

ADVANTAGES OF LEASING

The popularity and growth of leasing is best explained by its advantages. They include:

1. *Financing advantage* in the form of 100% financing at fixed rates and without a down payment and more flexible than debt agreements.
2. *Reduction of the risk of obsolescence* to the lessee that may include in some cases the transfer of the risk in residual value to the lessor.
3. *Tax advantages* through the deduction of the lease payments or a write-off of the full cost of the asset.
4. *Alternative minimum tax problems* may turn the alternative minimum tax (AMT) to our advantage. As explained by Kieso and Weygandt: "under the AMT rules, a portion of accelerated depreciation deduction are considered tax preference items that are added to a company's regular taxable income to arrive at the alternative minimum taxable income (AMTI). The company must pay whichever is higher, the regular tax or the AMT. Since ownership of equipment can contribute to an increase AMTI and, ultimately, to an alternative minimum tax liability in excess of the regular tax liabilities, companies often find leasing a way to avoid the owners alternative tax provisions.[4]
5. *Balance sheet advantages* through the absorption of an operating lease rather than a capitalized lease and therefore not adding a liability to the balance sheet and preserving a good borrowing capacity, a good rate of return, current ratio and ratio of debt to stockholders' equity.[5] The expensing of an operating lease constitutes a good form of "off-balance-sheet financing."

TYPES OF LEASES OF PERSONAL PROPERTY AND CRITERIA FOR CAPITALIZATION

As stated earlier, the lease that transfers substantially all the risks and benefits of ownership is essentially capitalized as an asset by the lessee and a sale by the lessor. FASB No. 13 identified four criteria applicable to both lessor and lessee and two criteria applicable only to the lessor to help in the classification of personal property leases.

The capitalization criteria applicable to both lessee and lessor are:

1. The lease transfers ownership of the property to the lessee.

2. There is a bargain purchase option in the lease contract.

3. The lease term is equal to 75% of the estimated economic life of the leased property.

4. The present value of the minimum lease payments (excluding executory costs) equals or exceeds 90% of the fair value of the leased property of the lessor.[6]

The capitalization criteria applicable to the lessor only are:

1. The collectibility of the minimum lease payments is reasonably predictable.

2. No important uncertainties surround the amount of unreimbursable costs yet to be incurred by the lessor under the lease.

Given the above criteria, the classification of the lessee is one of the following:

1. An *operating lease* if the lease does not meet any of the four criteria applicable to both lessee and the lessor.

2. A *capital lease* if the lease meets any of the four criteria applicable to both the lessee and lessor.

The classification by the lessor is one of the following:

1. A *sales-type lease* if (a) the lease meets one or more of the four criteria applicable to both the lessee and lessor, (b) the lease meets both of the criteria applicable to lessor only and (c) there is a manufacturer's or dealer's profit (or loss) to the lessor measured by the difference between the fair value of the leased property at the inception of the lease and the lessor's cost or carrying value (book value).

2. A *direct financing lease* if (a) the lease meets one or more of the four criteria applicable to both the lessee and lessor, (b) the lease meets both of the criteria applicable to the lessor only, and (c) there is no manufacturer's or dealer's profit (or loss) to the lessor.

3. An *operating lease* if the lease does not meet any of the four criteria applicable to both lessee and lessor and does not meet both the criteria applicable to the lessor.

ACCOUNTING FOR CAPITAL LEASE BY THE LESSEE

Important Elements of a Capital Lease

The computation and entries required in a capital lease depend on a good understanding of the following four elements:

1. *Minimum lease payments*: They are the payments accepted or required to be paid by the lessee to the lessor. They include the following:
   A. *Minimum rental payments* which are the minimum required payments by the lessee under the lease terms.
   B. *Guaranteed Residual Value* which is an estimated residual value of the leased property as guaranteed by the lessee or a third party, unrelated to the lessor. It is the amount that the lessor has the right to require the lessee to purchase the asset that the lessor is guaranteed to realize.[7]
   C. *Penalty on Failure to Renew or Extend* the lease that is sometimes required of the lessee.
   D. *Bargain Purchase Option* which is an option at the inception of the lease, to purchase the lease property at the end of the lease term at a fixed price sufficiently below the expected fair value to make the purchase reasonably assured.

2. *Executory Costs* which are the ownership-type costs, such as insurance, maintenance and tax expenses, to be excluded, if born by the lessee, from the computation of present value of the minimum lease payments.

3. *The Discount Rate* which is used in the computation of the present value of the minimum lease payments and included after:
   A. *The lessee's incremental borrowing rate* defined as: "the rate that, at inception of the lease, the lessee would have incurred to borrow the funds necessary to buy the leased asset on a secured loan with repayment terms similar to the payment schedule called for in the lease,"[8] or
   B. *The lessor's interest rate implicit in the lease* if known by the lessee and it is less than the lessee's incremental borrowing rate. It is the discount rate that equates the present value of the minimum lease payments and any unguaranteed residual value acquiring the lease to the fair value of the leased property to the lessor.[9]

Capital Lease by the Lessee Illustrated

A lease without a purchase or bargain purchase option (annuity due basis) is illustrated. The Zribi Company (lessor) and the Alvertos Company (lessee) sign a lease agreement on January 1, 1996, calling for the Zribi Company to lease Greek restaurant equipment to the Alvertos Company beginning January 1, 1996. The relevant information is as follows:

1. The lease term is five years. The lease is noncancellable and requires equal payments of $14,990.81 at the beginning of each year.
2. The equipment has a fair value and cost of $50,000, estimated life of five years and a zero residual value.
3. The Alvertos Company agreed to pay the executory costs of $3,000 per year, which are included in the annual payments to the Zribi Company.
4. There is no renewal option or purchase option, with the equipment reverting to the Zribi Company.
5. The Alvertos Company's incremental borrowing rate is 11% per year, the Zribi's implicit lease rate is 10% and is known to the Alvertos Company.

The lease meets two criteria for a classification as a capital lease, namely, (a) a lease term of five years equal to the equipment's economic life, and (b) a present value of lease payments of $50,000 (assigned below) that is higher than 90% of fair value of the equipment ($50,000). The capitalized amount as an asset is the present value of the minimum lease payments. It is computed as follows:

Capitalized amount = ($14,990.81 − $3,000) × 4.16986 (the present value of an annuity due for 5 periods at 10%) = $11,990.81 × 4.16986 = $50,000.

All the relevant information is computed in Exhibit 6.1. The journal entries are as follows:

1. Recording of the capital lease on January 1, 1996:
   Leased Equipment under Capital
   Leases $50,000
       Obligation under Capital
       Leases $50,000

The entry recognizes an asset and an obligation at the present value of rental payments ($50,000) rather than the total annual rental payments of $74,954.05 ($14,990.81 × 5).

2. Recording the first rental payment in advance on January 1, 1996:
   Property Taxes Expenses $3,000

Exhibit 6.1
Alvertos Company: Lease Amortization Schedule (Annuity Due Basis)

Date	Annual Lease Payment (a)	Executory Costs (b)	Interest at 10% on Unpaid Obligations (c)	Reduction of Lease Obligation (d)	Balance of Lease Obligation Liability (e)
1/1/96					$50,000.00
1/1/96	$14,990.81	$3,000	$------0------	$11,990.81	$38,009.19
1/1/97	$14,990.81	$3,000	$3,800.919	$ 8,189.891	$29,819.299
1/1/98	$14,990.81	$3,000	$2,981.929	$ 9,008.881	$20,810.418
1/1/99	$14,990.81	$3,000	$2,081.041	$ 9,909.769	$10,900.700
1/1/00	$14,990.81	$3,000	$1,090.064	$10,900.700	$-----0-----
	$74,954.05	$15,000.00	$9,953.953	$50,000.00	

(a) Required lease payments
(b) Executory costs paid by the lessee and included in rental payments
(c) Columns (e) at the beginning of the year × 10% except for 1/1/96
(d) (a) − (b) − (c)
(e) Preceding balance − (d)

Obligations under Capital Lease	$11,990.81	
Cash		$14,990.81

This entry recognizes (a) the executory costs of $3,000, (b) the principal (or reduction of the lease obligation) or $11,990.81 and (c) zero interest expense since no interest has accrued.

3. Recognition of accrued interest as of December 31, 1996:

Interest Expense	$3,800.919
Accrued Interest on Obligation under Capital Lease (or Interest Payable)	$3,800.919

The interest expense is recognized in the year it is accrued as a result of the applicable of the accrual concept.

4. Recognition of annual depreciation of leased equipment on December 31, 1996:

Deprecation Expense–Capital Leases	$10,000	
Accumulated Depreciation–Capital Leases		$10,000
($50,000/5 years)		

5. At the end of the year, the Obligation under Capital Leases on the balance sheet is divided into its current and noncurrent portion as follows:

   A. *Current Liabilities*

Interest Payable	$3,800.919
Obligations under Capital Leases	$8,185.891

   B. *Noncurrent Liabilities*

Obligation under Capital Leases	$29,819.891

6. Recording the second rental payment in advance January 1, 1997:

Property Tax Expenses	$3,000	
Accrued Interest on Obligation under Capital Lease	$3,800.919	
Obligation under Capital Lease	$8,189.851	
Cash		$14,990.81

7. The same pattern of entries is followed through the year 2000.

Operating Method of the Lessee Illustrated

If the capital lease between the Zribi Company and the Alvertos Company was in fact an operating lease then the rental payments will be recorded at the beginning of each year as follows:

Rent Expense	$14,990.81	
Cash		$14,990.81

No rent asset or corresponding liability is recognized in the balance sheet. Only rent expense is recognized in the income statement and a note disclosure is required for all operating leases that have noncancellable lease terms in excess of one year.

A comparison of the charges under the capital lease approach and the operating lease approach as shown in Exhibit 6.2, indicates that (a) the total charges are the same and (b) the charges are higher in the earlier years and lower in the later years under a capital lease. The use of capitalization under capital lease rather than expensing under an operation lease results in:

Exhibit 6.2
Alvertos Company: Charges to Operations, Capital Lease versus Operating Leases

	Capital Lease				Operating Lease Charges	Difference
Year	Depreciation	Executory Costs	Interest	Total Charge		
1996	$10,000.00	$3,000.00	$3,800.919	$16,800.919	$14,990.81	$1,810.109
1997	$10,000.00	$3,000.00	$2,981.929	$15,981.929	$14,990.81	$991.119
1998	$10,000.00	$3,000.00	$2,081.041	$15,081.041	$14,990.81	$90.231
1999	$10,000.00	$3,000.00	$1,090.064	$14,090.064	$14,990.81	$(900.746)
2000	$10,000.00	$3,000.00	$-----0-----	$13,000.000	$14,990.81	$(1,990.81)
	$50,000.00	$15,000.00	$9,953.953	$74,954.05	$74,954.05	$----0----

a. Higher short- and long-term debt because of the recognition of "Obligations under Capital Lease,"

b. Higher fixed assets because of the recognition of "Leased Equipment under Capital Leases," and

c. Lower income in the earlier years and higher income in the later years of the life of the lease.

ACCOUNTING FOR LEASES BY THE LESSOR

The lessor's interest in leases is related to the following three benefits:

1. *Interest Revenue.* Leasing is a form of financing, therefore financial institutions and leasing companies find leasing attractive because it provides competitive interest margins.

2. *Tax Incentives.* In many cases, companies that lease cannot use the tax benefit, but leasing provides them with an opportunity to transfer such tax benefits to another party (the lessor) in return for a lower rental rate on the leased asset.

3. *High Residual Value.* Another advantage to the lessor is the reversion of the property at the end of the lease term. Residual values can produce large profits.[10]

As explained earlier, the classification of leases by the lessor results in one of three types of leases: (a) operating lease, (b) sales-type lease or (c) direct financing lease.

Direct Financing Leases by the Lessor: Key Concepts

As explained earlier, a direct financing lease is a lease that meets one or more of the criteria applicable to both lessee and lessor, meets both of the criteria applicable to the lessor only and there is no profit or loss to the lessor. Because there is no profit and loss in a direct financing lease the net receivable to the lessor must equal the cost of carrying value of the property. Three accounts need to be defined:

1. *Lease Payments receivable or Minimum Lease Payments receivable*: This is the gross investment. It is equal to the sum of: (a) The undiscounted minimum lease payments to be received by the lessor plus (b) The unguaranteed residual value accruing to the lessor. Note that: (a) The "minimum lease payments" include: rental payments (excludes executory costs), a bargain purchase option (if any), a guaranteed residual value (if any) and penalty for failure to renew (if any); (b) The lease payments receivable includes either guaranteed or unguaranteed residual value. The guaranteed residual value is included in the minimum lease payments and the unguaranteed residual value is included as a second item.

2. *Unearned Interest Revenue or Unearned Interest Leases*: This is the difference between the gross investment or lease payment receivable and the cost or carrying value of the lease property.

3. *Net Investment to the Lessor*: This is the difference between the gross investment and the unearned interest revenue. Generally, the balance sheet treats the unearned interest revenue as a contra-account to be deducted from the Minimum Lease Payments Receivable to yield the "net investment to the lessor."

Direct Financing by the Lessor: Illustrated

Returning to the previous example between the Zribi Company and the Alvertos Company, the following information is relevant:

1. The five-year uncancellable lease beginning January 1, 1996, requires equal rental payments of $14,990.81 that include $3,000 of property costs.

2. The equipment has a cost and a fair value of $50,000, an estimated life of five years and no residual value.

3. No initial direct costs are included and no renewable options are included, with the property returning to the Zribi Company at the end of the lease.

4. Collectibility of payments is assumed and no unreimbursable costs are expected.

5. The interest rate implicit in the lease is 10%. It is the rate that, when applied to the gross receivable, will discount that amount to a present value that is equal to the net receivable. The annual rental payments charged to the lessor are computed as follows:

$$\text{Annual payments: } \frac{\text{Known Present Value Equal to the Cost of Equipment}}{\text{Present Value of an Annuity due of 1 for 5 periods at 10\%}}$$

$$= \frac{\$50,000}{4.16986} = \$11,990.81$$

6. The lease meets the criteria for a direct financing lease classification. It is a direct financing lease rather than a sales-type lease because the fair value (present value) of the property is equal to its cost.

7. The Lease Payments Receivable is equal to the minimum lease payments minus executory costs paid by the lessor plus the undiscounted unguaranteed residual value accruing to the lessor. Therefore:

$$\text{Lease Payments Receivable} = [(\$14,990.81 - \$3,000) \times 5] + \$0$$
$$= \$59,954.05$$

8. The Unearned Interest Revenue is equal to the minimum lease payment receivable minus the cost or carrying value of the leased equipment. Therefore:

$$\text{Unearned Interest Revenue} = \$59,954.05 - \$50,000 = \$9,954,05$$

9. The Net Investment to the lessor is equal to $50,000 the minimum lease payments receivable of $59,954.05 minus the Unearned Interest Revenue of $9,954.05.

10. The accounting entries based on the lease amortization schedule shown in Exhibit 6.3 are as follows:

A. Initial recording of the lease on January 1, 1996:
Lease Payments Receivable $59,954.05

Exhibit 6.3
Zribi Company: Lease Amortization Schedule (Annuity Due Basis)

Date	Annual Lease Payment (a)	Executory Costs (b)	Interest on Net Investment at 10% (c)	Net Investment Recovery (d)	Net Investment (e)
1/1/96					$50,000.00
1/1/96	$ 14,990.81	$3,000.00	$-----0-----	$11,990.81	$38,009.19
1/1/97	$ 14,990.81	$3,000.00	$3, 800.919	$ 8,189.891	$29,819.299
1/1/98	$ 14,990.81	$3,000.00	$2,981.929	$ 9,008.881	$20,810.418
1/1/99	$ 14,990.81	$3,000.00	$2,081.041	$ 9,909.769	$10,900.700
1/1/00	$ 14,990.81	$3,000.00	$1,090.064	$10,900.700	$-----0-----
	$ 75,954.05	$15,000.00	$9,953.953	$50,000.00	

(a) Required lease payments producing 10% return on net investment
(b) Executory costs paid by the lessee and included in the rental payments
(c) Column (e) at the beginning of the year × 10% (except for 1/1/96)
(d) (a) − (b) − (c)
(e) Preceding balance − (d)

Equipment	$50,000
Unearned Interest Revenue-	
Leases	9,954.05

B. Collection of first year's lease payment in January 1, 1996
Cash	$14,990.81
Lease Payment Receivable	$11,990.81
Property Tax Expense/	
Property Taxes Payable	$3,000

C. Recognition on December 31, 1996 of interest revenue earned during the first year:
Unearned Interest Revenue-	
Leases	$3,800.919
Interest Revenue-Leases	$3,800.919

The unearned interest revenue is amortized by the use of the effective interest method. At the end of the year 1996 the lease payments receivable is disclosed as both current and noncurrent assets as follows:

1. The net investment at the end of 1996 is equal to $41,810.109 (the balance of 1/1/96 of $38,009.19 plus the interest receivable for 1996 of $3,800.919)

2. The current portion ($14,990.81) is the net investment to be received in 1997 of $8,189.891 plus the interest of $3,800.919

3. The noncurrent portion is the $29,819.299 [lease payments] receivable of $35,972.43 ($11,990.81 × 3) minus unearned interest revenue of $6,153.054 ($1,090.064 + $2,081.041 + $2,981.919)

   D. Collection of second year's
   lease payments:

Cash	$14,990.81	
Lease Payment Receivable		$11,990.81
Property Tax Expense/		
Payable		$3,000.00

   E. Recognition of December 31, 1997 interest revenue earned during the year:

Unearned Interest Revenue-		
Leases	$2,981.929	
Interest Revenue-Leases		$2,981.929

   F. The entries should be similar through the year zero.

Operating Method by the Lessor: Illustrated

The lessor using the operating method proceeds by (a) recording every rental payment as a rental revenue, (b) recording a depreciation expense for the leased equipment and (c) recording other additional costs as expense. Returning to the previous example between the Zribi Company and the Alvertos Company, the following entries are made:

A. Collection of rental payment on operating lease on January 1, 1996

Cash	$14,990.81	
Rental Revenue		$14,990.81

B. Recognition of Annual Depreciation expense on December 1, 1996

Depreciation Expense-Leased		
Equipment	$5,000	
Accumulated Depreciation-		
Leased Equipment		$5,000

IMPACT OF RESIDUAL VALUE

Residual value is the estimated fair value of the leased asset at the end of the lease, and can be either guaranteed or unguaranteed by the lessee. As stated earlier, guaranteed residual values are included in the

Exhibit 6.4
Zribi's Computation of Lease Payments in the Case of a Residual Value (Lessor's Computation) (Annuity Due Basis)

1. Fair Market Value of Equipment of the Zribi Company	$50,000.00
2. Less Present Value of Residual Value ($2,500 X 0.62092)	$ 1,552.30
3. Amount to be Recovered by the Zribi Company	_____
Through the Lease Payments	$48,447.70
4. Five Periodic Lease Payments ($48,447.70/4.16986)	$11,618.543

minimum lease payments. Both guaranteed and unguaranteed residual values affect accounting by the lessee and lessor. For the lessor the determination of the lease payments with a residual value is also different. For example, let's suppose that the Zribi Company expected the Greek restaurant equipment to have a residual value of $2,500. It would compute the lease payments as shown in Exhibit 6.4.

The Case of a Guaranteed Residual Value

The guaranteed residual value is included in the minimum lease payments which require that the lessee capitalize the present value of the amount guaranteed. To illustrate, let's return to the Zribi Company as the lessor and the Alvertos Company as the lessee example and assume that the Alvertos Company agrees to guarantee the entire amount of the residual value of $2,500. The capitalized amount for the Alvertos Company is as follows:

1. Present value of five annual rental payments discounted at 10% ($11,618.543 × 4.16986)

    $48,447.70

Plus

2. Present value of a single sum of $2,500 (the guaranteed residual value) discounted at 10% ($2,500 × 0.62092) $1,552.30

Exhibit 6.5
Alvertos Company: Lease Amortization Schedule (Lessee's Computation);
Annuity Due Basis and Guaranteed Residual Value (GRV)

Date	Lease Payment Plus GRV (a)	Executory Costs (b)	Interest at 10% on Unpaid Obligation (c)	Reduction of Lease Obligation (d)	Balance of Lease Obligation Liability (e)
1/1/96					$50,000.00
1/1/96	$14,618.543	$ 3,000	$----0----	$11,618.543	$38,381.457
1/1/97	$14,618.543	$ 3,000	$ 3,838.145	$ 7,780.398	$30,601.059
1/1/98	$14,618.543	$ 3,000	$ 3,060.105	$ 8,558.438	$22,042.621
1/1/99	$14,618.543	$ 3,000	$ 2,204.262	$ 9,414.281	$12,628.34
1/1/00	$14,618.543	$ 3,000	$ 1,262.834	$10,355.709	$ 2,272.631
12/31/00	$ 2,500.000		$ 227.263	$ 2,272.03*	$-----0-----
	$75,592.715	$15,000	$10,592.609*	$50,000.00*	

*rounded
(a) Required lease payments
(b) Executory costs paid by the lessee and included in rental payments
(c) Column (e) at the preceding balance × 10% except for 1/1/96
(d) (a) − (b) − (c)
(e) Preceding balance − (d)

3. Present value of minimum lease payments
$50,000.00

The Alvertos Company lease amortization schedule is shown in Exhibit 6.5. It is the basis for the following entries:

1. Capitalization of lease on January 1, 1996.
   Leased Equipment under Capital
   Leases $50,000
       Obligation under Capital
       Leases $50,000
2. First rental payment on January 1, 1996
   Property Tax Expense $3,000.00
   Obligations under Capital Leases $11,618.543
       Cash $14,618.543

3. Recognition of accrued interest on December 31, 1996

Interest Expense	$3,838.145	
Interest Payable		$3,838.145
(or Accrued Interest		
Obligation under Capital		
Leases)		

4. Recognition of the annual depreciation of leased equipment on December 31, 1996.

Depreciation Expense-Capital		
Leases	$9,500.00	
Accumulated Deprecation–		
Capital Leases		$9,500.00
[($50,000 − $2,500) /5 years]		

5. At the end of the year 1996, the Obligation Under Capital Leases in the balance sheet is divided into its current and noncurrent portions as follows:

A. Current Liabilities

Interest Payable	$3,838.145
Obligations under Capital Leases	$7,780.398

B. Noncurrent Liabilities

Obligations under Lease	$30,601.059

6. Recording the second rental payments in advance January 1, 1997

Property Tax Expense	$3,00.00	
Obligations under Capital Leases	$7,780.398	
Accrued Interest on Obligations		
under Capital Leases	$3,838.398	
Cash		$14,618.543

7. The same patterns of entries are followed through the year zero

The Case of an Unguaranteed Residual Value

The lessee does not recognize the unguaranteed residual value in the computation of the minimum lease payments and the capitalization of the leased asset under obligation. To illustrate, let's return to the Zribi Company as the lessor and the Alvertos Company as the lessee example and assume that the Alvertos Company does not agree to guarantee the entire amount of the residual value of $2,500. The capitalized amount for the Alvertos Company is as follows:

1. Present value of five annual rental payments discounted at 10%

Exhibit 6.6
Alvertos Company: Lease Amortization Schedule (Lessee's Computation); Annuity Due Basis and Unguaranteed Residual Value

Date	Lease Payments (a)	Executory Costs (b)	Interest at 10% on Unpaid Obligations (c)	Reduction of Lease Obligation (d)	Balance of Lease Obligation Liability (e)
1/1/96					$48,447.70
1/1/96	$14,618.543	$3,000	$-----0-----	$11,618.543	$36,829.152
1/1/97	$14,618.543	$3,000	$3,682.915	$ 7,935.628	$28,893.529
1/1/98	$14,618.543	$3,000	$2,889.352	$ 8,729.191	$20,164.338
1/1/99	$14,618.543	$3,000	$2,016.433	$ 9,602.11	$10,562.228
1/1/00	$14,618.543	$3,000	$1,056.222	$10,562.22*	$-----0-----
	$73,092.715	$15,000	$ 9,644.922	$48,447.70*	

*Rounding error

($11,681.543 × 4.16986) $48,447.70

Plus

2. Unguaranteed residual value of $2,500 not capitalized
                                          $———0———

3. Present value of minimum lease payments
                                            $48,447.70

The Alvertos Company lease amortization schedule is shown in Exhibit 6.6. It is the basis for the following entries:

1. Capitalization of lease on January 1, 1996
    Leased Equipment under Capital
    Leases $48,447.70
        Obligation under Capital
        Leases $48,447.70

2. First rental payment on January 1, 1996
    Property Tax Expense $3,000.00
    Obligations under Capital Leases $11,618.543
        Cash $14,618.543

3. Recognition of accrued interest on December 31, 1996
    Interest Expense $3,682.915

Interest Payable $3,682.915

4. Recognition of annual depreciation expense on December 31, 1996
   Depreciation Expense–Capital
   Leases $9,689.54
      Accumulated Depreciation–
      Capital Leases $9,689.54
      ($48,447.70/5 years)

5. At the end of the year 1996 the Obligation under Capital Leases in the balance sheet is divided into its current and noncurrent portions as follows:
   A. Current Liabilities
      Interest Payable $3,682.915
      Obligations under Capital
      Leases $7,935.628
   B. Noncurrent Liabilities
      Obligation under Capital
      Leases $28,893.529

6. Recording the second rental payment on January 1, 1997
      Property Tax Expense $3,000.00
      Obligations under Capital
      Leases $3,682.915
      Accrued Interest on
      Obligations under
      Capital Leases $7,935.628
      Cash $14,618.543

7. The same patterns of entries are followed through the year zero.

The Case of a Residual Value for the Lessor

For the lessor the assumption is that the residual value will be realized whether it is guaranteed or unguaranteed. Returning to the previous example of the Zribi Company as the lessor and the Alvertos Company as the lessee and the residual value of $2,500 (whether guaranteed or unguaranteed), the following information is relevant to the lessor:

1. Gross Investment: ($11,618.543 × 5) + $2,500 = $60,592.715

2. Unearned interest revenue:
   $60,592.715 − $50,000 = $10,592.715

3. Net Investment = $60,592.715 − $10,592.715 = $50,000.00

Exhibit 6.7

Zribi Company: Lease Amortization Schedule (Lessor's Computation); Annuity Due Basis and Guaranteed Residual Value (GRV)

Date	Lease Payment Plus GRV (a)	Executory Costs (b)	Interest at 10% on Net Investment (c)	Net Investment Recovery (d)	Net Investment
1/1/96					$50,000.00
1/1/96	$14,818.543	$3,000	$-----0-----	$11,618.543	$38,381.457
1/1/97	$14,818.543	$3,000	$ 3,838.145	$ 7,780.398	$30,601.059
1/1/98	$14,818.543	$3,000	$ 3,060.105	$ 8,558,438	$22,042.621
1/1/99	$14,818.543	$3,000	$ 2,204.262	$ 9,414.281	$12,628.34
1/1/00	$14,818.543	$3,000	$ 1,262.834	$10,355.709	$ 2,272.631
12/31/00	$ 2,500.00	$3,000	$ 227.263	$ 2,272.03*	$-----0----
	$75,592.715	$15,000	$10,592.609*	$50,000.00*	

*rounded
(a) required lease payments
(b) Executory costs paid by the lessee and included in rental payments
(c) Column (e) at the preceding balance × 10% except for 1/1/96
(d) (a) − (b) − (c)
(e) Preceding balance − (d)

The lease amortization schedule for the lessor is illustrated in Exhibit 6.7. It is the basis of the following entries:

1. Initial recording of the lease at its inception on January 1, 1996
   Lease Payments Receivable $60,592.715
        Equipment $50,000.00
        Unearned Interest Revenue–
        Leases $10,592.715

2. Recording of first rental payment on January 1, 1996
   Cash $14,618.543
        Lease Payments Receivable $11,618.543
        Property Tax Expense/
        Property Tax Payable $3,000.00

3. Recognition of accrued interest on December 31, 1996
   Unearned Interest Revenue-
   Leases $3,838.145
        Interest Revenue-Leases $3,838.145

SALES-TYPE LEASES: ACCOUNTING FOR THE LESSOR

The major difference between a direct financing lease and a sales type lease is the presence of a manufacturer's or dealer's profit or loss in a sales-type lease and the accounting for initial direct costs. This profit or loss is equal to the difference between:

1. The present value of the minimum lease payments (net of executory costs) computed at the interest rate implicit in the lease (i.e., the sales price), and

2. The cost or carrying value of the asset plus any initial direct costs less the present value of the unguaranteed residual value accruing to the benefit of the lessor.

To illustrate a sales-type lease, let's assume the same example as in direct financing where (a) the residual value is $2,500 (with a present value of $1,553.30), (b) the equipment had a cost of $40,000 to the lessor, the Zribi Company and (c) the fair market value of the residual value is $1,000.

A. The following information is relevant to the lessee in case the residual value is a guaranteed residual value:
   1. Gross Investment: ($11,618.543 × 5) + $2,500 = $60,592.715
   2. Unearned Interest Revenue: $60,592.715 − $50,000 = $10,592.715
   3. Sale Price of the Asset: ($48,447.70 + $1,552.30) = $50,000.00
   4. Cost of Goods Sold: $40,000
   5. Gross Profit: ($50,000 − $40,000) = $10,000

B. The following information is relevant to the lessor in case of an unguaranteed residual value:
   1. Gross Investment: ($11,618.543 × 5) + $2,500 = $60,592.715
   2 Unearned Interest Revenue: $60,592.715 − $50,000 = $10,592.715
   3. Sale Price of the Asset: $48,447.70
   4. Cost of Goods Sold: $40,000 − $1,552.30 = $38,447.70
   5. Gross Profit: ($48,447.70 − $38,447.70) = $10,000.00

C. The entries assuming guaranteed residual value are:
   1. Initial recording of the sales-
      type lease on January 1, 1996

Minimum Lease Receivable	$60,592.715	
Cost of Goods Sold	$40,000.00	
Sales Revenue		$50,000.00
Equipment Held for Lease		$40,000.00
Unearned Interest Leases		$10,592.715

2. Collection of annual payment on January 1, 1996

Cash	$14,618.543	
Minimum Lease Receivable		$11,618.543
Property Expense/Payable		$3,000.00

3. Recognition of interest revenue on December 31, 1996

Unearned Interest-Leases	$3,682.915	
Interest Revenue		$3,682.915

4. Collection of second annual payment for January 1, 1997

Cash	$14,618.543	
Minimum Lease Receivable		$11,618.543
Property Expenses/Payable		$3,000.00

5. Recognition of interest revenue as of December 31, 1997

Unearned Interest-Leases	$2,889.352	
Interest Revenue		$2,889.352

6. Recognition of residual value at the end of lease term (December 31, 2000)

Equipment	$1,000.00	
Cash	$1,500.00	
Lease Payment Receivable		$2,500.00

D. The entries assuming an unguaranteed residual value are:

1. Initial recording of the sales-type lease on January 1, 1996

Minimum Lease Receivable	$60,592.715	
Cost of Goods Sold	$38,447.70	
Sales Revenue		$48,447.70
Equipment		$40,000.00
Unearned Interest Revenue		$10,592.715

2. Collection of annual payment for January 1, 1996

Cash $14,618.543		
Minimum Lease Receivable		$11,618.543
Property Tax Expense/		
Payable		$3,000.000

3. Recognition of interest revenue on December 31, 1996

Unearned Interest-Leases	$3,682.915	
Interest Revenue		$3,682.915

4. Collection of second annual payment for January 1, 1997

Cash	$14,618.543	
Minimum Lease Receivable		$11,618.543
Property Tax Expense/		
Payable		$3,000.000

5. Recognition of interest revenue on December 31, 1997

Unearned Interest-Leases	$2,889.352	
Interest Revenue		$2,889.352

6. Recognition of residual value at the end of the lease term (December 31, 2000)

Equipment	$1,000.00	
Cash	$1,500.00	
Lease Payment Receivable		$2,500.00

ACCOUNTING FOR INITIAL DIRECT COSTS BY THE LESSOR

Initial direct costs have been redefined in FASB Statement No. 91.[11] Basically, the initial direct costs of a lease transaction include two types, as follows: (1) Incremental direct costs as the costs resulting from the lease and are essential to the lease transaction; (2) Internal direct costs are the costs related to the evaluation of the lessee's personal condition, and other costs of the activities performed by the lessor.

The accounting treatment for initial direct costs is different for each type of lease:

1. For an operating lease, the initial direct costs are recorded as prepaid assets and allocated over the lease term as an expense proportionally to the rental receipts.
2. For a direct financing lease, the initial direct costs are deferred and added to the net investment in the leases and amortized over the life of the lease as a yield adjustment.
3. For a sales-type lease, the initial direct costs are expensed in the same period.

ACCOUNTING FOR SALE-LEASEBACK

A sale-leaseback occurs when the owner of the asset sells the asset to another and simultaneously leases it back from the buyer to (a) benefit from better financing and (b) derive a tax advantage from deducting the entire lease payment. Two situations are possible:

1. If the lease meets the condition for a capital lease, the profit from the transaction is deferred and amortized over the lease term by the lessee in proportion to the amortization of the leased asset.
2. If the lease does not meet the conditions for a capital lease, it is considered an operating lease and the profit is amortized proportionally to the rental payments.

Any loss, however, is recognized immediately. To illustrate a sale-leaseback transaction, assume that the Lessee Corporation, on January 1, 1996, sells a ship having a book value of $2,460,000 to the Lessor Corporation for $10,460,000 and simultaneously leases it back under the following conditions:

1. The term of the lease is four years, noncancellable.
2. The payments at the beginning of every year are of $3,000,000.
3. The fair value of the ship is $10,460,000 on January 1, 1996, with a four-year economic life.
4. The lessor's rate is 10%.

Assuming the lease is a capital lease, the entries based on Exhibit 6.8 are as follows:

1. Sale of ship by the lessee to the lessor on January 1, 1996

Cash	$10,460,000	
Ship		$2,460,000
Unearned Profit on Sale-		
Leaseback		$8,000,000

2. Initial recording of sale-leaseback on January 1, 1996

Leased Ship under Capital Leases	$10,460,000	
Obligations under Capital		
Leases		$10,460,000

3. Recording of first lease payment on January 1, 1996

Obligations under Capital Leases	$3,000,000	
Cash		$3,000,000

4. Recording of depreciation expense on December 31, 1996

Depreciation Expense	$2,615,000	
Accumulated Depreciation		
($10,460,000/4)		$2,615,000

5. Amortization of unearned profit on sale-leaseback on December 31, 1996

Unearned Profit on Sale-		
Leaseback	$2,000,000	
Realized Profit on Sale-		
Leaseback		
(or Depreciation Expense-		
Leased Ships)		
($8,000,000/4)		$2,000,000

Exhibit 6.8
Lessee's Lease Amortization Schedule

Date	Annual Rental Payment	Interest at 10%	Reduction of Balance	Balance
1/1/96				$10,460,000
1/1/96	$3,000,000.00	$-----0-----	$3,000,000	$ 7,460,000
1/1/97	$3,000,000.00	$746,000	$2,254,000	$ 5,206,000
1/1/98	$3,000,000.00	$520,000	$2,480,000	$ 2,726,000
1/1/99	$3,000,000.00	$272,000	$2,726,000	$-----0-----

6. Recognition of interest expense on December 31, 1996
   Interest Expense $746,000
        Interest Payable $746,000

To the lessor the entries are as follows on January 1, 1996

1. Ship $10,460,000
        Cash $10,460,000
2. Lease payments Receivable ($3,000,000 × 4) $12,000,000
        Ship $10,000,000
        Unearned Interest Revenue $2,000,000
3. Cash $3,000,000
        Lease Payments Receivable $3,000,000

ACCOUNTING FOR LEASES INVOLVING REAL ESTATE

There are specific issues for accounting for leases involving real estate
that include lease of land only, lease of both land and building and lease
of real estate and equipment.

A. If the lease involves land only, the lease for the lessee is a capital
lease if (a) there is a transfer of ownership and (b) there is a bargain
purchase option; otherwise it is an operating lease. For the lessor the
lease is either a sale-type or a direct financing lease if it meets the ownership conditions, the bargain purchase option condition and the collectibility and uncertainty tests. Otherwise it is an operating lease.

B. If the lease involves both land and building and meets the ownership conditions and the bargain purchase option conditions, it is a capital lease for the lessee and either a sale-type lease or a direct financing lease for the lessor depending on the existence of a profit or loss.

C. If the lease involves both land and building, does not meet the ownership conditions and the bargain purchase option conditions, and the fair value of the land and buildings is less than 25% of the fair value of both the land and buildings, the land portion is ignored and the lease is classified on the basis of the building characteristics.

D. If the lease involves both land and building, does not meet the ownership condition and the bargain purchase option condition, and the fair value of the land is more than 95% of the fair value of both land and buildings, both the lessee and the lessor account for the land as an operating lease and the building as a capital lease if it meets the necessary requirements.

E. If the lease involves both real estate and equipment, the portion of the minimum lease payments applicable to the equipment portion of the lease should be estimated by whatever means are appropriate. The classification of the equipment is done separately from the real estate. The accounting for the real estate portion proceeds as described in the preceding section. For a leased property which is part of a large building, "reasonable estimates of the lease property's fair value might be objectively determined by referring to an independent appraisal of the lease property or to estimated replacement cost information."[12]

NOTES

1. "Accounting for Leases," *FASB Statement No. 13 as Amended and Interpreted through January 1990* (Norwalk, Conn.: FASB, 1990), Sec. 1.10.101.

2. John H., Myers, "Reporting of Leases in Financial Statements," *Accounting Research Standard No. 4* (New York: AICPA, 1964).

3. Yuji Ijiri, *Recognition of Contractual Rights and Obligations*, Research Report (Stamford, Conn.: FASB, 1980).

4. Donald E. Kieso and Jerry J. Weygandt, *Intermediate Accounting*, 4th ed. (New York: John Wiley & Sons, 1993), p. 1123.

5. E. A. Imhoff, Jr., R. C. Lipe, and D. W. Wright, "Operating Leases: Impact of Constructive Capitalization," *Accounting Horizons* (March 1991).

6. "Accounting for Leases," par. 7.

7. Ibid.

8. "Accounting for Leases," par. 5(1).

9. Ibid., par. 5(k).

10. Kieso and Weygandt, *Intermediate Accounting*, p. 1133.

11. "Accounting for Nonrefundable Fees and Costs Associated with Originating or Acquiring Loans and Initial Direct Costs of Leases," *FASB Statement of Financial Accounting Standards No. 91* (Stamford, Conn.: FASB, 1987).

12. "Leases Involving Only Part of a Building," *FASB Interpretation No. 24* (Stamford, Conn.: FASB, 1978), par. 6.

7

Segmental Reporting

The growth of conglomerate multinational corporations, international accounting and/or international trade has led to a need for segmental reporting. Rather than being limited to a reporting of financial position, performance and conduct of the whole firm, segmental reporting would add specific reporting of the activities of identifiable and reportable segments of the firm. There was, in addition, an international call for such reporting as firms expanded beyond their domestic activities to generate revenues and perform operations outside the borders of their parents' countries. Therefore, diversification, added to the internationalization of the firms, presented an opportunity for change in the framework of accountability and disclosure toward a combination of aggregate and less aggregate forms of reporting. Like all reporting issues, segmental reporting generated a debate about its implementation, the nature of accounting standards, its impact on users in the market and its potential predictive ability. This chapter elaborates on the various aspects of this debate and its international and managerial ramifications.

NATURE OF SEGMENTAL REPORTING

Firms have been reacting to their environments by adopting new organizational structures based on decentralization and the development or acquisition of domestic or foreign segments. What results is a more diversified company. Robert K. Mautz offers the following definition of a diversified company:

A company which is either so managerially decentralized, so lacks operational integration, or has such diversified markets that it may experience rates of profitability, degrees of risk, and opportunities for growth which vary within the company to such extent that an investor requires information about these variations in order to make informed decisions.[1]

What appears from this definition is that first the phenomenon of diversification emanates from management decentralization, a lack of operational integration, or activity in diverse markets; and second that the differences in the financial profits of the segments call for segmental reporting deemed useful to investors.

Segmental reporting consists, therefore, in providing relevant information about segments. It can be rationalized within the "Fineness Theorem" of the information economics literature.[2] It implies that the information system$_{n1}$ is said to be "as fine as" the information system$_{n0}$ if $_{n1}$ is a "subpartition" of$_{n0}$; that is, if each data set of$_{n1}$ provides a partitioning of the states of nature which is at least as detailed (or as "fine") as that present in the data sets of$_{n0}$. Applied to segmental reporting, it implies that the information system obtained by segmental reporting and consolidated data together is "finer" than the disclosure of consolidated data alone. The fineness argument does not, however, consider the incremental costs required by the additional disclosure. Roseanne M. Mohr elaborates as follows:

It must be noted, however, that the costs of the "finer" disclosures could impair the theoretical result. Although the gathering and reporting costs associated with segmental disclosure may be small (due to the use of similiar data in managerial decision contexts), externalities and practical data limitations would still impose greater cost. For example, competitive reactions or managerial reluctance to adopt "risky" projects may affect the expected payoff to the decision maker. Furthermore, uncertainty about data reliability and comparability would inhibit the use of the incremental disclosure of segment earnings data, wherein differences in cost determination methods and in common cost allocation schemes can influence the reported amounts.[3]

EVALUATION OF SEGMENTAL REPORTING

Use of Segmental Reporting

The use of segmental reporting had been on the increase even before the international standard setters made some calls for it. Attitudinal studies of preparers and users in the United States showed at the time an expressed interest in the dissemination of segmental reporting. These studies include one on financial analysts and commercial bankers by Morton Backer and Walter B. McFarland,[4] and one on financial analysts and corporate executives by Mautz.[5] Another attitudinal study by J. Cramer reported some of the perceived problems of segmental reporting experienced by corporate controllers, namely, in defining the segments, the restrictions on data comparability that might result from the use of different cost allocation and transfer pricing techniques; and finally, the externality costs associated with the development of auditing standards, the increased legal exposure of managers and auditors and the reaction of competitors.[6]

S. J. Gray and Lee H. Radebaugh examined the extent of geographical information provided in practice in the United States and the United Kingdom, and the significant differences in the nature and content of disclosures between countries both in terms of voluntary disclosures and those required by accounting standards.[7] Given the greater flexibility in the applications of regulations governing segment disclosures in the United States as well as reduced scope in terms of the amount of information to be disclosed, it is not surprising that their findings indicate that U.S. firms disclose more segment information, especially with respect to intraenterprise sales, profits and assets. In the case of employees, however, the increased emphasis on employee reporting in the United Kingdom may explain the greater disclosure of employee information in the United Kingdom. An interesting result was that U.S. firms disclosed fewer geographic segments than did the U.K. firms, and a higher level of aggregation. The following explanation was provided:

One final note relates to the demand of investors for information, U.K. segment disclosure practices are determined by the London Stock Exchange and, therefor, its investors. This has resulted in more segments than for U.S. firms, as summarized above, but certainly not in more information per segment. Large MNE's (Multinational enterprises), such as those in this study, actively use the international markets to raise debt as well as equity capital, so they effectively compete with each other for capital. In spite of this, the more extensive information required of U.S. MNEs has not resulted in U.K. firms trying to match U.S. firms in terms of disclosure. It is evident that the Capital market has not insisted on this information from U.K. firms, leading one to question the necessity of the fuller range of U.S. disclosure.[8]

Gray also examined the European experience with segmental reporting and found that U.K.–based companies exhibited greater disclosure of business analyses of profits and geographical analyses of sales and profits.[9] Factors explaining the differences included managerial (corporate strategy, organizational structure and cost and competitive aspects), legal and political, professional and stock market and investment environments. Two variables were singled out as more important: the structure of the company with respect to the extent of its economic integration and managerial coordination, and the differential stimulus to disclosure provided by the regulatory environment of legal, professional and stock market requirements. According to Gray:

the impact of the formal variable is difficult to assess from company reports, and further research into the aspect would seem useful to determine the feasibility of disclosure. With regards to the impact of the latter variable, there is little doubt about the unsatisfactory nature of existing disclosure requirements, such as they are. The critical problem is that of defining appropriate criteria for the identification of reportable segments. This is a difficulty which is currently thwarting the developement of segment reporting in the EEC, given that a case for providing such information is perceived to exist by some of the rule-making bodies concerned.[10]

Evaluation of Segmental Reporting

Various arguments have been made with regard to segmental reporting since business concerns began to grow and acquire a multisegmental characteristic.

The usefulness of segmental reporting was linked generally to (a) the informational content of the information in terms of the profitability, risk and growth of the different segments of a firm, and (b) the relevance to users in their assessment of the earnings potential and the risk of company as a whole, to governments in their developement of public policy positions on multinational and/or large companies and to management encouraging a corporate strategy. This last point is raised as follows:

Managerial efficiency may be promoted by the attention to corporate strategy that the publication of segmented reporting will encourage. Management may also be concerned to evaluate their internal management control system. The provision of segmental reports will necessitate managerial evaluation of cost allocation procedures and the bases on which transfer prices between segments are calculated. Perhaps the most important spur to efficiency could be the increased competition that may result from segmental disclosures with consequent benefits to the economy as a whole. The effect of this may be exaggerated, however, as all companies will be similarily placed. But it may at least redress to some extent the competitive disadvantage experienced by the unitary company, with no business or geographical diversification, as compared to the multibusiness-multinational company whose operations have become progressively complex and whose financial statements have become correspondingly opaque.[11]

Naturally, as in all accounting issues, not all arguments are in favor of segmental reporting. Not only is the usefulness of segmental reporting questioned when compared to the role of consolidated data, but also the costs of disclosure are raised as a subject of concern. The question is whether the cost of segmental disclosure could serve to offset the theoretical benefits of "finer" information systems. There is undoubtedly limited evidence with regard to the cost aspects of segmental disclosure, in addition to the lack of evidence on information-processing issues, data-reliability considerations and externality costs. There is also the problem of the lack of comparability when "(i) apparently similar segments in different firms may be identified differently, (ii) the treatment of inter-segment transfers may differ, and (iii) common costs may be allocated over different bases.[12]

THE U.S. POSITION ON SEGMENTAL REPORTING

Official Pronouncements

The U.S. position on reporting financial information by segment is mainly expressed in FASB Statement No. 14, Financial Reporting for Segments of a Business Enterprise. Other applicable authoritative statements include Statements 18, 21, 24, 30 and 69, and technical bulletins 79–4, 79–5 and 79–8. FASB Statement No. 14 requires public companies whose securities are publicly traded or which are required to file financial statements with SEC to include disaggregated information about operations in various industries, foreign operations, export sales and sales to major companies. FASB Statement No. 221, Suspension of the Reporting of Earnings Per Share and Segment Information by Nonpublic Enterprises, exempts nonpublic firms from the provisions of FASB Statement No. 14. Similarily, FASB Statement No. 24, Reporting Segment Information in Financial Statements That are Presented in Another Enterprise's Financial Report, exempts the reporting entity whose consolidated

financial statements contain separable financial statements in the following circumstances:

1. The separable financial statements are also consolidated or combined in a
   complete set of financial statements and both sets of financial statements are
   included in the same financial reports;
2. The separable financial statements are those of a foreign investee (not a
   subsidiary) of the primary reporting unit, and the separable financial statements do not follow the provisions of SFAS No. 14; or
3. The separable financial statements are those of an investee accounted for
   using the cost or equity method.

Therefore, SFAS No. 21 and No. 24 affect the applicability of SFAS
No. 14, by putting forth limitations.

Because SFAS No. 14 differentiates between domestic and foreign
operations, the following presentation will make the same differentiation.

Domestic Operations

In SFAS No. 14 an industry segment is defined as a component of an
enterprise, engaged in providing a product or service, or a group of
related products and services, primarily to unaffiliated customers for a
profit. The first requirement of SFAS No. 14 is the determination of the
industry segments that need to be reported separately. The three-step
procedure goes as follows: First, the company should identify sources of
revenue (by product or service rendered) on a worldwide basis for entity;
second, the company should group related products and services into
industry segments. Three factors from paragraph 100 of SFAS No. 14
are to be considered in determining industry segment as follows:

1. The nature of a product. Related products have similiar purposes or end uses.
   Thus, they may be expected to have similar rates of profitability, similiar
   degrees of risk, and similar opportunities for growth.
2. The nature of the production process. Sharing of common or interchangeable
   production or sales facilities, equipment, labor force, or service group or use
   of the same or similar basic raw materials may suggest that products or
   services are related. Likewise, similar degrees of labor intensiveness or similar degrees of capital intensiveness may indicate a relationship among products or services.
3. Markets and marketing methods. Similarity of geographic marketing areas,

types of customers, or marketing methods may indicate a relationship among products or services. The sensitivity of the market to price changes and to changes in general economic conditions may indicate whether products and services are related or unrelated.

Third, the company should determine the reporting segments. Six tests are suggested to facilitate the decision, namely, the revenue test, the profitability test, the assets test, the comparability test, the dominance test and the explanation test. These tests are applied as follows:

The revenue test requires that the segment revenue be 10% or more of the combined revenue (sales to unaffiliated customers and intersegment sales or transfers) of all the enterprise's industry segments. Segment revenue is calculated as follows:

$$SR = S + IS + INTO + INTR$$

where

SR = segment revenue,
S = sales to unaffiliated customers,
IS = intersegment sales and transfers,
INTO = interest income from sources outside of the firm,
INTR = interest income from intersegment notes receivable.

The profitability test requires that the absolute of the segment's operating profit or loss be 10% or more of the greater, in absolute amount, of (a) the combined operating profits of all industry segments that did not incur an operating loss or (b) the combined operating losses of all industry segments which did incur an operating loss. The operating profit or loss is segment revenue less operating expenses except the following items:

1. Any revenues earned at the corporate level and not related to any segment
2. General corporate expenses
3. Interest expense, except if segment operations are primarily of a financial nature
4. Domestic and foreign income taxes
5. Equity in earnings of unconsolidated subsidiaries or investees
6. Extraordinary items
7. Gains or losses on discontinued operations

8. Minority interest

9. Cumulative effect of changes in accounting principles

The asset test requires, if the segment fails both preceding tests, that the identifiable assets of the segments be 10% or more of the combined segment identifiable assets. Identifiable assets include tangible and intangible assets net of valuation allowances used by the industry segment and the allocated portions of the assets used by two or more segments. Assets that are intended for general corporate purposes are excluded.

The comparability test requires that the segment be reported separately if management feels such a treatment is needed to achieve interperiod comparability.

The test of dominance requires that the segment not be reported separately if it can be classified as dominant. A dominant segment should represent 90% or more of the combined revenues, operating profits or losses and identifiable assets, and no other segment meets any of the 10% tests.

The explanation test determines whether a substantial portion of an enterprise's operations is explained by its segment information. The combined total of the revenue from reportable segments must be 75% or more of all revenue from sales to unaffiliated customers. If combined revenues do not meet this test, additional segments must be added until the test is met.

The following example illustrates the application of operational tests.

Segment	Unaffiliated Revenue	Intersegment Revenue	Total Revenue	Operating Profit (Loss)	Identifiable Assets
U	50	50	100	10	50
V	100		100	10	40
W	150	100	250	(20)	100
X	200		200	10	150
Y	250	50	300	(100)	100
Z	300		300	100	80
	$1,050		$1,250	$10	$520

Revenue Test: (10%) ($1,250) = $125
    Reportable segments: W, X, Y, Z

Operating Profit or Loss Test: (10%) ($130) = $13

    Reportable Segments: W, Y, Z,

    Because total operation profit
    ($130) is greater than the operat-
    ing loss ($120), total operating
         profit is used as the base.

Identifiable Assets Test: (10%) ($520) = $52

    Reportable segments: W, X, Y, Z

Explanation Test: (75%) ($1,050) = $787.50

    Segments W, X, Y and Z have
    total unaffiliated revenues of
    $900, which is greater than
    $787.50. Therefore, the
    explanation test is met and no
    additional segments need to be
    reported.

In conclusion, given the above tests and the number of reportable segments does not exceed ten and that there is no dominant segment, the
reportable segments are W, X, Y, and Z.

Following the choice of the reportable segments, SFAS No. 14 suggests specific disclosure requirements using one of the three methods:
(1) In financial statements, with reference to related footnote disclosures,
(2) in the footnotes to financial statements, (3) in a supplementary schedule, which is not part of the four financial statements.

The information to be reported in the reportable segments includes the
following:

1. Revenue information including (a) sale to unaffiliated customers, (b) intersegment sales or transfers, along with the basis of accounting for such sales
   or transfers, and (c) a reconciliation of both sales to unaffiliated customers
   and intersegment sales or transfers on the consolidated income statement

2. Profitability information

3. Identifiable assets information

4. Other disclosures including the aggregate amount of depreciation, depletion and amortization; the amount of capital expenditures; equity in unconsolidated but vertically integrated subsidiaries and their geographic location; the effect of a change in accounting principle on segment income, the type of products and services produced by each segment, specific accounting policies, the basis used to price intersegment transfers, the method used to allocate common costs, and the nature and the amount of any unusual or infrequent items added to or deducted from segment profit.

Foreign Operations

SFAS No. 14 requires separate disclosure of domestic and foreign activities. Foreign operations are those revenue-generating activities that are located outside the enterprise's home country and are generating revenue either from sales to unaffiliated customers or from intraenterprise sales or transfer between geographic areas.

Two tests may be used to determine if foreign operations are to be reported separately: (a) revenue from sales to unaffiliated customers is 10% or more of consolidated revenue as reported in the firm's income statement and (b) identifiable assets of the firm's foreign operations are 10% or more of consolidated total assets as reported in the firm's balance sheet. After a foreign operation has been determined to be reportable, it must be added to foreign operations in the same geographic area. Geographic areas are defined as individual countries or groups of countries as may be determined as appropriate in the firm's circumstances. The following factors are to be considered in grouping foreign operations: proximity, economic affinity, similarities in business environment, and nature, scale and degree of interrelationship of the firm's operations in the various countries. The disclosure requirements for foreign operations are similar to those for domestic operations.

Export Sales and Sales to Major Customers

Export sales are those sales made by a domestic segment to unaffiliated customers in foreign countries. If export sales amount to 10% or more of the total sales to unaffiliated customers, they should be separately disclosed in the aggregate and by such geographic areas considered appropriate.

Similarily, if 10% or more of the revenue of a firm is derived from a single customer, a separate disclosure is required along with the segments making the sale. SFAS No. 30, "Disclosure of Information About Major Customers," identifies the following entities as being a single customer to comply with the 10% test: a group of entities under common control, the federal government, a state government, a local government or a foreign government.

INTERNATIONAL POSITIONS

In the United Kingdom the 1981 Companies Act requires segmental reporting in the financial statements, stating specifically:

If in the course of the financial year, the company has carried out a business of two or more classes that, in the opinion of the directors, differ substantially from each other, there shall be stated in respect of each class (desciding it): (a) the amount of the turnover attributable to that class, and (b) the amount of the profit or loss of the company before taxation which is in the opinion of the directors attributable to that class.

In addition, the act calls for a disclosure of turnover by geographic areas when the firm has been supplying different markets. The disclosure is generally made in the director's report.

The Canadian position is more comprehensive. It is expressed in Section 1700 of the Canadian Institute of Chartered Accountants (CICA) handbook. The requirements of the section are, in general, similar to the provision of SFAS No. 14. The only exception relates to the required disclosure of information about major customers of the firm. While the exposure draft preceding Section 1700 called for this information, it was later deleted from the final version.

The international position in segment reporting was reported in August 1981 by the release of IAS No. 14, Reporting Financial Information by Segments, by the International Accounting Standards Committee. It basically suggests the following disclosures for each reported industry and geographic segment: (a) sales or other operating revenues, distinguishing between revenue derived from customers outside the firm and revenue derived from other segments, (b) segment results, (c) segment assets employed, expressed either in monetary amounts or as percentages of the consolidated totals, and (d) the basis for intersegment pricing. The reportable segments are referred to as economically significant entities, defined as those subsidiaries whose levels of revenues, profits, assets, or employment are significant in the countries in which their major operations are conducted.

With regard to the European Economic Community (EEC), one of the provisions of the fourth directive requires turnover only to be analyzed by activity and geographic segment.

In Australia there is no requirement to disclose segment information except disclosure of the extent to which each corporation in a group contributes to consolidated profit or loss.

Segmental reporting is also recommended in the OECD guidelines for multinational corporations[13] and in the U.N. proposals for accounting and reporting by multinational corporations.[14]

PREDICTIVE ABILITY OF SEGMENTAL REPORTING

The predictive ability of segmental information has been examined in several studies. In the first study, William R. Kinney, Jr., tested the relative predictive power of subentity earnings data for a sample of firms which have voluntarily reported sales and earnings data by subentity. He found that the predictions were on the average more accurate than predictions based on models using consolidated performance data alone.[15]

In the second study, Daniel W. Collins extended and updated the preliminary work of Kinney using data disclosed under the line-of-business reporting requirements initiated by the SEC.[16] The SEC had required, beginning December 31, 1970, that all registrants engaged in various segments report sales and profits before taxes and extraordinary items by product line in their annual 10-K report. Collins's findings corroborated Kinney's earlier findings, suggesting that "SEC product line revenue and profit disclosures together with industry sales projections published in various government sources provide significantly more accurate estimates of future total-entity sales and earnings than the procedures that rely totally on consolidated data."[17]

The third study focused on the predictive ability of U.K. segment reports. C. R. Emmanual and R. H. Pick confirmed in a U.K. setting the earlier findings that segmental disclosure of sales and profits data is useful in providing more accurate predictions of corporate earnings.[18] They also suggested more research with the predictive ability paradigm.

Future studies may prove rewarding in not only determining whether disclosure is worthwhile, but also what form it should take if the predictions are to become more accurate. Two contenders in this respect are segment reports presented in terms of an industrial/geographical segment matrix and the measurement of segment earnings in terms of contribution instead of profit before tax. This would allow national industrial growth forecasts to be accommodated in the segment-based models while the use of contribution would avoid the possibly significant distorting effects of transfer pricing and common cost allocations. Given the availability of data, the predictive ability criterion may prove more useful in gauging the most appropriate form which segmental disclosure should follow.[19]

Finally, P. Silhan provided no evidence that consistently supported the predictive superiority of either the "Consolidated" or the "Segmental" earnings data.[20] His study differed from the earlier research in two important aspects: (a) the earnings forecast models are based on the use of Box Jenkins time series analysis and (b) the use of stimulation approach permitting an examination of the effect of the number of segments on predictive accuracy.

Related studies examined the accuracy of published earnings forecasts in conjunction with segmental reporting. Both R. M. Barefield and E. Cominsky[21] and B. Baldwin[22] were able to show a relationship between the forecast accuracy and the presence of segmental reporting indicating that the availability of segmental data could improve the accuracy of analyst's earnings projections.

A position evaluation of these results was stated as follows:

In summary, the studies addressing the accuracy of analysts' forecasts have utilized a variety of research techniques and have provided evidence that improved earnings predictions can accompany the disclosure of segmental data. Within the context of segmental reporting, improved accuracy of forecasts may be viewed as one of the "benefits" implicit in the theoretical "fitness" result. But the earnings forecast studies have also provided some evidence with regard to another "fineness" comparison. Specifically, no predictive improvements beyond those associated with the availability of segmental sales were obtained when segmental earning amounts were added to the data set. Such a finding directs attention toward the desirability of testing for the decision effects of segmental earnings in other contexts and assessing the costs of this added disclosure.[23]

USERS' PERCEPTIONS OF SEGMENTAL REPORTING

The early research investigated the "real world" perceptions of segment reporting and provided evidence showing users' and preparers' interest in the production and dissemination of segment sales and earning data. Those studies relying mostly on survey data include Backer and McFarland,[24] Mautz[25] and Cramer.[26] The other studies used controlled experiments to evaluate the impact of segmental disclosure on individual decision making. The first study was by J. C. Stallman.[27]

The second study was by Richard F. Ortman.[28] He asked financial analysts to assign a per-share offering price to each diversified firm, one that included segmental data and one that did not. The firms were expected to go public in the immediate future. The results showed that with segmental data the value of each firm's stock was in accordance with the present value of its expected return as reflected by industry average P/E ratios, and without segmental data the reverse was experienced. He concluded as follows: "The decrease in the variance with regard to the distributions of the per-share values of the diversified firms' stocks in this study may mean that segmental disclosure by all such firms could result in greater stability in the movement of prices of these firms' stocks. The results of this study strongly suggest that diversified firms should include segmental data in their financial reports."[29]

This result could not, however, be taken as conclusive evidence of the impact of segmental reporting on users. As stated by Mohr: "Ortman's selected industries (auto parts and office/computer equipment), and the radical changes in industry involvement that were revealed only in the segmental data, could have driven the observed results."[30]

MARKET PERCEPTIONS OF SEGMENTAL REPORTING

Various market-based studies examined the association between segmental reporting and mean returns on stocks. Twombly found no evidence of statistically significant differences between the mean return vector of the experimental portfolios (partitioned by segmental disclosure level and industry concentration) with the mean return vector of the control portfolios (partitioned by industry concentration only).[31] He concluded that "the event of a firm's disclosure of both segment revenues and profits provided no unanticipated information to the capital market, whether the disclosures were conditional upon the market concentration or not.[32]

Because Twombly's study was limited to an examination of mean returns on stock of firms engaged in voluntary segmental reporting, Ajinka decided to conduct a comprehensive empirical evaluation of the proposition that "the SEC's LOB (line of business) earnings disclosure requirement . . . enabled market participants to reassess the risk-return characteristics of conglomerate firms."[33] His results were, however, consistent with those reported by Twombly. A similar attempt by Horowitz and Kolodny provided similar evidence.[34] This evidence was, however, based on portfolio, and the individual effects may be largely neutralized at the portfolio level. Other strategies were also tried. For example, Foster examined the association between residual returns and the good and bad "news" aspects of segmental disclosure in the insurance industry.[35] His finding indicated that return-assessments effects could be associated with the disclosure of a segmental data set. Similarily, R. F. Kochanek examined whether the predictive aspects of good versus poor quality segmental disclosure could influence the timing of market return assessments.[36] This evidence supported a relationship between return assessment, earnings prediction and the disclosure of a segmental data set incorporating (at a minimum) segmental sales amounts.

Finally, Bimal K. Prodhan examined the impact of segmental geographic disclosure on the systematic risk profile of British Multinational Firms, showing an association between the two variables and the finding that the onset of a geographic segmental disclosure is more likely to be abrupt than gradual.[37] Prodhan argued that his findings would provide some more evidential input to the debate on segmentation of the international capital market, known as the Grubal-Agmon controversy.[38] He makes the point as follows: "Since geographical information is associated with beta changes it can be said that the international capital markets are likely to be segmented, since an integrated international capital market share is unlikely to be a benefit from diversification across countries."[39]

Collins, however, tested the efficiency of the securities market and provided somewhat mixed evidence with respect to the assessment of segmental data on security returns.[40]

PUSH-DOWN ACCOUNTING

Nature of Push-Down Accounting

Push-down accounting has been defined as "the establishment of a new accounting and reporting basis for an entity in its separate financial statements, based on a purchase transaction in the voting stock of the entity that results in a substantial change of ownership of the outstanding voting stock of the entity."[41]

The definition requires that the cost to the acquiring entity in a business combination accounted for by the purchase method be computed to the acquired entity. In other words, the valuation of the acquired entities, assets, liabilities and stockholders' equity should be derived from the purchase transaction. The value paid for the stock by the investor is "pushed down" as the new basis for the net assets of the acquired firm.

Push-down accounting is certainly an ideal subject for definite pronouncements from the international standard-setting bodies. APB Opinion No. 16 does not address push-down accounting in the separate financial statements of acquired entities. It provides principles for the acquiring entity to assign values to the assets and liabilities of the acquired entity but does not address whether those new values should be reflected in the separate statements of the acquired entity. An authoritative book on auditing discusses the concept of the push-down theory as follows:

The principle for recording asset values and goodwill in the accounts of the company to reflect the purchase of its stock by another entity or group of stockholders has been called the "push-down" theory. At present, the question of how far should it be carried is unanswered. . . . Until all of the ramifications of the push-down theory are fully explored, we would prefer to see its implementation limited to 100 percent (or nearly 100 percent—the pooling theory's 90 percent would be a good precedent) transaction.[42]

Some of the standard setters have attempted to provide some guidance for the implementation of push-down accounting. The SEC, in Staff Accounting Bulletin (SAB) No. 54, expressed the view that push-down accounting should be required when the subsidiary is "substantially" wholly owned, with no publicly held debt or preferred stock, should be encouraged when the subsidiary has public debt or preferred stock that was outstanding when it became substantially wholly owned, and should not be required when there is an already existing large minority in the subsidiary. Another regulator, the Federal Home Loan Bank Board (FHLBB), which charters and supervises federal savings and loan associations and is empowered to establish policies and issue regulations for them related to dividend rates, lending and other aspects of operations, in its January 17, 1983, Memorandum R55, made push-down accounting acceptable provided at least 90% of the stock is acquired and is found in accordance with GAAP (generally accepted accounting principles) by the auditor.

The situation is not better in other countries. In Canada, for example, the CICA handbook does not provide definite guidance. Paragraph 3060.01 refers to the carrying value of fixed assets stating in part: "The writing up of fixed assets values should not occur in ordinary circumstances. It is recognized, however, that there may be instances where it is appropriate to reflect fixed assets at values that are different from historical costs, e.g., at appraised values assigned in a reorganization."

The decision of the Canadian preparer rests on whether a specific purchase can be defined as "ordinary circumstances"; otherwise a reevaluation of assets and liabilities is called for.

Historical Cost versus Push-Down Accounting

The difference between historical cost and push-down accounting can best be illustrated by a simple example. Let's suppose that an investor buys a firm in a leveraged buyout transaction, one in which a firm is acquired largely with borrowed funds. To secure the transaction the investor paid $5,000 and borrowed $10,000 to acquire 100% of the firm's outstanding stock. The estimated fair market value of the firm's property and equipment, found to be $8,000 by the appraisers, was to be reduced by $7,000 for GAAP purposes to reflect the differences between market values and the tax basis.

Exhibit 7.1 shows the financial statements of both the historical cost and the push-down approach. Under the historical cost approach the balance sheet appears relatively stronger with a positive stockholders' equity account and a much stronger debt/equity ratio. In addition, the fixed assets under push-down accounting reflect the fair values paid for by the purchase of the stock.

Evaluation of Push-Down Accounting

The rationale for push-down accounting is that a new basis for accounting for the acquired firm would provide information that is more relevant to financial statement users. The substance of the transaction resulting from a total change of ownership is equivalent to the purchase of the net assets of the business and, therefore, the fair value paid for the purchase of the stock should be reflected in the balance sheet. In addition, symmetry in presentation is deemed necessary. First, separate

Exhibit 7.1
Historical Cost versus Push-Down Accounting

	Historical Cost		Push-Down	
	Before Purchase	After Purchase	Push Down Entities	Purchase Taxes
Current Assets	$ 2,000	$ 2,000	--	$ 2,000
Fixed Assets	5,000	5,000	$ 2,000[1]	7,000
Goodwill			10,000[2]	10,000
Total Assets	$ 7,000	$ 7,000		$ 19,000
Current Debt	$ 1,500	$ 1,500	--	$ 1,500
Long-Term Debt	2,500	12,500	10,000[3]	12,500
Total Debt	$ 4,000	$ 14,000	10,000	$ 14,000
Common Stock	$ 2,000	$ 7,000	(2,000),[4] $5,000[5]	$ 5,000
Retained Earnings	1,000	1,000	(1,000)	--
	$ 3,000	$ 8,000	$ 2,000	$ 5,000
Treasury Stock	--		--	--
Stockholders' Equity (Deficit)	$ 3,000	$ (7,000)	$ 2,000	$ 5,000
Total	$ 7,000	$ 7,000		$ 19,000

[1]To adjust to tax basis value.
[2]Purchase accounting adjustments per APB Opinion No. 16 = ($15,000 − $5,000).
[3]To increase the long-term debt by the amount of borrowing.
[4]To record purchase of outstanding shares.
[5]To record equity financing for acquisition.

financial statements of subsidiary companies should be based on the purchase price of the entity because that is the basis required in consolidated
financial statements. Second, SFAS No. 14 requires that separate segmental information reflect the parent's cost basis for each segment. Although not every subsidiary is a segment, the symmetry condition calls
for a similar presentation in the separate financial statement. "Issuing

separate financial statements on a basis other than push-down could result in the distribution of some conflicting financial information for the same segment or subsidiary."[43]

Opponents of the method would agree that push-down accounting is a current valuation method which violates the historical cost basis of accounting. It disregards the separate entity assumption, affects, comparability, and may lead to violations of agreements. In addition, there is no logical method of determining which stockholder transactions would qualify for a push-down. In other words, what percentage of ownership is required for legitimizing a push-down? Published examples seem to follow 100% change in ownership. The SEC staff bulletin requires push-down accounting when a subsidiary is "substantially" wholly owned. The FHLBB memorandum called for at least a 90% change in ownership. Finally, the AICPA's task force members unanimously agreed on 51% change in ownership as being inappropriate. In fact, the AICPA's task force identified some strong arguments against push-down accounting:

- Transactions of an entity's stockholders are not transactions of the entity and should not affect the entity's accounting.
- A new basis of accounting would be detrimental to interests of holders of existing debt and nonvoting capital stock who depend on comparable financial statements for information about their investments and do not have access to other financial information. Push-down accounting would affect the ability of the entity to comply with debt covenants required by outstanding debt and would materially alter the relationships in the entity's financial statements. When minority owners and other investors are entitled to financial statements, those financial statements should be prepared based on transactions of that entity and not transactions of stockholders.
- FASB Statement No. 14 deals with reporting information on segments of a business and is irrelevant to push-down accounting.
- There is no logical way to establish limits for determining which owner's transactions should qualify for push-down accounting.[44]

The AICPA task force also raised pertinent questions about the desirability of push-down accounting in case of split-offs or spin-offs and concluded that it was not desirable. There was, however, an agreement that if a new basis is established in a series of step transactions, it should be consistent with the parent's basis determined under the rules for the purchase method of accounting.

Other issues of importance were not raised by the task force. Examples include the following:

• If a company proposes to sell a number of subsidiaries (or a division), is it appropriate to use push-down accounting basis for presenting divisional statements that will be subject of sale negotiations? Can this be considered in accordance with GAAP or an acceptable alternative disclosed basis of accounting?

• Where the purchase price on a corporation's acquisition is determined by future results, when is the appropriate time to establish the entity's fair market value—at the moment of acquisition or on determining the ultimate purchase price? Should historical values be used until the final purchase price is known?[45]

CARVE-OUT ACCOUNTING

Many multinational companies eager to raise huge amounts of cash have tended to sell off portions of subsidiaries, which became known as "carving out" subsidiaries. By doing so, they began tapping an uncommon source of financing—their equity in wholly owned subsidiaries. As stated by Schiff: "The lure is particularly strong when the subsidiary is operating in one of the popular industries on Wall Street or is experiencing impressive growth. In such cases, the parent can command a significant premium per share over its investment, and therefore can attract return. When deciding which subsidiary to sell, the natural choice is one operating in an industry whose stock is selling at high price-earnings ratios."[46]

To make the offerings attractive, some of these companies do not show the true cost of the unit. The true cost of the business is likely to be hidden because companies put subsidiary expenses on the books of the parent company. The bottom line for the parent is the same because its profits and losses include those of the subsidiaries. However, the subsidiaries' profits look better than they really are, which allows the parent company to sell the subsidiaries' stock at a much higher price than it is really worth. To stop this process and let the public know the true costs (and profits) of the subsidiaries, the SEC in 1983 issued Staff Accounting Bulletin (SAB) No. 55, "Allocation of Expenses to Subsidiaries, Divisions, and Lesser Business Components." The clear position was that the historical income statements of the subsidiary should reflect all of its costs of doing business, including those incurred by their parent company on their behalf.

Examples of such expenses are:

1. Officer and employer salaries
2. Rent or depreciation
3. Advertising
4. Accounting and legal services
5. Other selling, general, and administrative expenses
6. Interest and income tax expenses

In addition, SAB No. 55 requires that in those situations where expenses applicable to a subsidiary cannot be identified, they must be allocated on some reasonable basis, with appropriate footnote disclosure of the allocation method and management's assertion that such method is reasonable. How effective was SAB No. 55? Schiff states:

SAB 55 has resulted in more information disclosures of the relationship between a parent and its subsidiaries when they are issuing stock. The required disclosures put the subsidiary on a standalone basis and help the SEC carry out its mission to seek full and fair disclosure. If the practice of carving out subsidiaries persists as a financing technique, the reporting requirements will also evolve and become more uniform. Negotiated agreements will probably increase in popularity as a "basis" for allocating costs because of their certainty and simplicity in resolving the issue of parent-provided services.[47]

NOTES

1. Robert K. Mautz, *Financial Reporting by Diversified Firms* (New York: Financial Executives Research Foundation, 1968).

2. J. Marschak and R. Radner, *Economic Theory of Teams* (New Haven, Conn.: Yale University Press, 1971), pp. 53–59.

3. Roseanne M. Mohr, "The Segmental Reporting Issue: A Review of Empirical Research," *Journal of Accounting Literature* (Spring 1983), pp. 41–42.

4. Morton Backer and Walter B. McFarland, *External Reporting for Segments of a Business* (New York: National Association of Accountants, 1968).

5. Mautz, *Financial Reporting by Diversified Firms.*

6. J. Cramer, "Income Reporting by Conglomerates," *Abacus* (August 1968), pp. 17–26.

7. S. J. Gray and Lee H. Radebaugh, "International Segment Disclosures

by U.S. and U.K. Multinational Enterprises: A Descriptive Study," *Journal of Accounting Research* (Spring 1984), pp. 351–60.

8. Ibid., pp. 359–60.

9. S. J. Gray, "Segment Reporting and the EEC Multinationals," *Journal of Accounting Research* (Autumn 1978), pp. 242–53.

10. Ibid., pp. 252–53.

11. Sidney J. Gray, "Segmental or Disaggregated Financial Statements," in *Developments in Financial Reporting*, ed. Thomas A. Lee (London: Philip Allan, 1981), pp. 31–32.

12. Ibid., p. 33.

13. Organization for Economic Cooperation and Development (OECD), *International Investment and Multinational Enterprises* (Paris: OECD, 1979).

14. United Nations (UN), *International Standards for Accounting and Reporting for Transnational Corporations* (New York: UN, 1977).

15. William R. Kinney, Jr., "Predicting Earnings: Entity vs. Subentity Data," *Journal of Accounting Research* 9 (Spring 1971), pp. 127–36.

16. Daniel W. Collins, "Predicting Earnings with Sub-Entity Data: Some Further Evidence," *Journal of Accounting Research* (Spring 1976), pp. 163–77.

17. Ibid., p. 216.

18. C. R. Emmanual and R. H. Pick, "The Predictive Ability of UK Segment Reports," *Journal of Business Finance and Accounting* (Summer 1980), pp. 201–18.

19. Ibid., p. 216.

20. P. Silhan, "Stimulated Mergers of Existent Autonomous Firms: A New Approach to Segmentation Research," *Journal of Accounting Research* 20 (Spring 1982), pp. 255–62.

21. R. M. Barefield and E. Cominsky, "Segmental Financial Disclosure by Diversified Firms and Security Prices: A Comment," *Accounting Review* 50 (October 1975), pp. 818–21.

22. B. Baldwin, "Line-of-Business Disclosure Requirements and Security Analyst Forecast Accuracy," D.B.A. diss., Arizona State University, 1979.

23. Mohr, "The Segmental Reporting Issue," pp. 31–52.

24. Backer and McFarland, *External Reporting for Segments of a Business.*

25. Mautz, *Financial Reporting by Diversified Firms.*

26. Cramer, "Income Reporting by Conglomerates," pp. 17–26.

27. J. C. Stallman, "Toward Experimental Criteria for Judging Disclosure Improvement," *Empirical Research in Accounting: Selected Studies, 1969*, supplement to *Journal of Accounting Research* 7 (1969), pp. 29–43.

28. Richard F. Ortman, "The Effects on Investment Analysis of Alternative Reporting Procedure for Diversified Firms," *Accounting Review* 50 (April 1975), pp. 298–304.

29. Ibid., p. 304.

30. Mohr, "The Segmental Reporting Issue."

31. J. Twombly, "An Empirical Analysis of the Information Content of Segment Data in Annual Reports from an FTC Perspective," in *Disclosure Criteria and Segment Reporting*, ed. R. Barefield and G. Holstrom (Gainesville: University of Florida Press, 1979), pp. 56–96.

32. Ibid., p. 304.

33. B. Ajinka, "An Empirical Evaluation of Line of Business Reporting," *Journal of Accounting Research* 18 (Autumn 1980), pp. 343–61.

34. B. Horowitz and R. Kolodny, "Line of Business Reporting and Security Prices: An Analysis of an SEC Disclosure Rule," *Bell Journal of Economics* 8 (Spring 1977), pp. 234–49.

35. G. Foster, "Security Price Revaluation Implications of Sub-Earnings Disclosure," *Journal of Accounting Research* 13 (Autumn 1975), pp. 283–92.

36. R. F. Kochanek, "Segmental Financial Disclosure by Diversified Firms and Security Prices," *Accounting Review* 49 (April 1974), pp. 245–58.

37. Bimal K. Prodhan, "Geographical Segment Disclosure and Multinational Risk Profile," *Journal of Business Finance and Accounting* (Spring 1986), pp. 15–37.

38. J. Grubal, "Internationally Diversified Portfolios: Welfare Gains and Capital Flows," *American Economic Review* (1968), pp. 1299–1314; T. Agmon, "The Relationship among Equity Markets," *Journal of Finance* (May 1972), pp. 839–55.

39. Prodhan, "Geographical Segment Disclosure," p. 31.

40. D. Collins, "SEC Product-Line Reporting and Market Efficiency," *Journal of Financial Economics* (June 1975), pp. 125–64.

41. American Institute for Certified Public Accountants (AICPA), "Push-Down Accounting," Issues Paper by the Task Force on Consolidation Problems, Accounting Standards Division, New York, October 30, 1979.

42. P. L. Defliese, H. R. Jaenicke, J. D. Sullivan, and R. A. Gnospelius, *Montgomery's Auditing* (New York: John Wiley & Sons, 1984), p. 692.

43. AICPA, "Push-Down Accounting," p. 14.

44. Ibid., pp. 16–17.

45. James M. Sylph, "Push-Down Accounting: Is the U.S. Lead Worth Following?" *Canadian Chartered Accounting Magazine* (October 1985), p. 55.

46. Jonathon B. Schiff, "Carving Out Subsidiaries: Uncommon Financing and New Disclosure Requirements," *Corporate Accounting* (Spring 1986), p. 73.

47. Ibid., p. 75.

SELECTED READINGS

Barefield, R. M., and E. Cominsky. "Segmental Financial Disclosure by Diversified Firms and Security Prices: A Comment." *Accounting Review* 50 (October 1975), pp. 818–21.

Collins, Daniel W. "Predicting Earnings with Sub-Entity Data: Some Further Evidence." *Journal of Accounting Research* (Spring 1976), pp. 163–77.

Mautz, Robert K. *Financial Reporting by Diversified Firms*. New York: Financial Executives Research Foundation, 1968.

Mohr, Roseanne M. "The Segmental Reporting Issue: A Review of Empirical Research." *Journal of Accounting Literature* (Spring 1983), pp. 41–65.

8

Accounting for Foreign Currency Transactions and Futures Contracts

INTRODUCTION

Multinational firms engage mostly in transactions that are denominated in a foreign currency. The value of these transactions is affected by changes in exchange rates. These rates change every day. Accounting for foreign currency transactions needs to take account of these changes in values.

Multinational firms attempt to protect their trades in various commodities by entering into future contracts. Accounting for these contracts needs to account for all the characteristics of these contracts and the complexities associated with them.

This chapter examines the accounting treatments associated with each one of the two phenomena affecting the activities of multinational firms, namely: (1) accounting for foreign currency transactions and (2) accounting for future contracts.

ACCOUNTING FOR FOREIGN CURRENCY TRANSACTIONS

Foreign currency transactions require settlement in a currency other than the functional currency of the reporting entity. The functional currency of an entity is the currency used in the economic environment in which that entity operates. Statement of Financial Accounting Standards (SFAS) No. 52 covers the accounting treatments required for accounting for foreign currency transactions. In what follows, these treatments are presented within two major categories: accounting for foreign currency transactions that are not the result of forward-exchange contracts, and accounting for foreign currency transactions involving forward-exchange contracts.

Foreign Currency Transactions Not Involving Forward-Exchange Contracts

For those foreign currency transactions not involving forward-exchange contracts, the following treatments apply.

1. At the time of the transaction, the asset, liability, revenue or expense is recorded in the functional currency of the recording entity by use of the current exchange rate on the transaction.
2. At the balance sheet date and at the date of the settlement of the foreign currency translation, recorded balances in the foreign currency transaction accounts are adjusted to reflect the current exchange rate.
3. With two exceptions, gains and losses resulting from the restatement are reflected in the current period's income statement.
4. The two exceptions are foreign currency transactions that are the result of an economic hedge of a net investment in a foreign entity, and long-term, intercompany foreign currency transactions when the entities to the transaction are consolidated, combined or accounted for by the equity method in the reporting enterprise's financial statements. In both cases, the gains and losses are reported as translation adjustments in a separate component of the stockholders' equity account.

The two examples that follow illustrate these treatments. In Example 1, the treatment of transaction gains and losses in current net income is discussed in relation to the export and import of goods. Example 2 uses an intercompany foreign currency transaction to illustrate the treatment of transaction gains and losses as translation adjustments to stockholders' equity.

Example 1: Foreign Exchange Transaction Involving Imports or Exports of Goods

The American National Company, a domestic entity with a December 31, 19X3 year-end, sold merchandise to a foreign company on December 15, 19X3 for FC500,000 at 'net 30' terms. The following exchange rates are in effect on the following dates:

December 15, 19X3: FC1 = $0.50

December 31, 19X3: FC1 = $0.60

January 15, 19X3: FCI = $0.80

The accounting entries for this transaction follow:

1. At the date of the foreign exchange transaction, December 15, 19X3,

Accounts Receivable	$250,000	
Sales		$250,000

to record the sale of goods for $250,000 (FC500,000 × 0.50).

2. At the balance sheet date, December 31, 19X3,

Accounts Receivable	$50,000	
Exchange Gain		$50,000

to record the exchange gain of $50,000 (FC500,000) ($0.60 − $0.50). This exchange gain will be included in the 19X3 income statement of the American National Company, as a nonoperative item.

3. At the date of this settlement, January 15, 19X4,

Cash	$400,000	
Exchange Gain		$100,000
Accounts Receivable		$300,000

to record the amount received on settlement, equal to $400,000 (FC500,000 × $0.80) and the exchange gain of $100,000 (FC500,000 × ($0.80 − $0.60)).

Example 2: Foreign Exchange Transactions Involving Intercompany Items

On November 20, 19X3, the American National Company made an advance of FC800,000 to the Other National Company, which is a subsidiary of the American National Company. The advance is long-term in nature and is not expected to be repaid this year. Information about the exchange rates between the U.S. dollar and the foreign currency of the subsidiary is as follows:

November 20, 19X3: FC1 = $0.80

December 31, 19X3: FC1 = $0.95

The entries for this foreign exchange transaction follow:

1. At the date of the foreign exchange transaction, November 20, 19X3,
   Investment in Other National
   Company $640,000
       Cash $640,000
2. At the balance sheet date, no exchange gains and losses are recognized in
   the current net income, but instead enter into the determination of the translation adjustment as a component of stockholders' equity, as determined by
   the following:
   Amount used in translation
   adjustment = FC800,000
   ($0.95 −$0.80) = $40,000

Foreign Currency Transactions Involving Forward-Exchange Contracts

A *forward-exchange contract* is defined as an agreement to exchange different currencies at a specified date and at a specified rate (the forward rate). Firms enter into a forward-exchange contract with a third-party broker to guarantee a fixed exchange for the transaction. Three adjustments have to be computed and accounted for:

1. *Gain or loss (whether or not deferred) on a forward contract.* It is equal to the foreign currency amount of the forward contract multiplied by the difference between the spot rate at the balance sheet date and the spot rate at the inception of the forward contract (or the spot rate last used to measure a gain or loss on that contract for an earlier period).
2. *Discount or premium on a forward contract.* This discount is equal to the foreign currency amount of the contract multiplied by the difference between the contracted forward rate and the spot rate at the contract inception date.
3. *Gain or loss on a speculative forward contract.* This is equal to the foreign currency amount of the contract multiplied by the difference between the forward available for the remaining maturity of the contract and the contract forward rate (or the forward rate last used to measure a gain or loss on that contract for an earlier period).

The accounting treatment for a foreign currency transaction involving foreign exchange contracts can be handled in different ways, depending on whether the forward-exchange contract is intended as a hedge of an identifiable foreign currency commitment, a hedge of an exposed net-asset or liability position, or a hedge of a foreign currency speculation.

A forward-exchange contract is considered a hedge of an identifiable commitment if (1) the foreign currency transaction is designated as, and is effective as, a hedge of foreign currency commitment and (2) the foreign currency commitment is firm. In such a case, the gain on the forward contract will be deferred and accounted for in the cost basis of the object of the foreign currency commitment. Any loss is recognized currently rather than deferred. In addition, the discount premium on a forward contract will be deferred and included in the cost basis.

A forward-exchange contract that serves as a hedge of an exposed net-asset or liability position is accounted for in a different manner. The gain or loss is recognized in the current accounting period, while the discount or premium is accounted for separately over the life of the contract.

A forward-exchange contract that serves as a hedge of foreign currency speculation is also accounted for differently, with all gains and losses, premiums and discounts recognized currently.

The examples that follow involve the hedge of an identifiable foreign currency commitment, the hedge of an exposed net-asset or liability position, and the hedge of a foreign currency speculation to illustrate these treatments.

Example 1: Hedge of an Identifiable Foreign Currency Commitment

On December 10, 19X3, the American National Company agreed to buy merchandise from a foreign supplier (the Foreign National Company) for FC800,000 at "net 90" terms. At the same time, on December 10, 19X3, the American National Company entered into a forward-exchange contract for the delivery of FC800,000 in 90 days. The following exchange rates are in effect on the following dates:

December 10, 19X3, Forward Rate: FC1 = $0.60
December 10, 19X3, Spot Rate: FC1 = $0.50
December 31, 19X3, Spot Rate: FC1 = $0.55
March 10, 19X3, Spot Rate: FC1 = $0.65

Because the contract qualifies as an identifiable foreign currency commitment, the entries are as follows:

1. At the date of inception of the forward-exchange contract, December 10, 19X3:

Foreign Currency Receivable from Exchange Broker	$400,000	
Premium of Forward-Exchange Contract	$80,000	
Payable to Exchange Broker		$480,000

to record the receivable and the payable relating to the forward-exchange contract. The premium is equal to ($0.60 − $0.50) × FC 800,000.

2. At the balance-sheet date, December 31, 19X3,

Foreign Currency Receivable from Exchange Broker	$40,000	
Deferred Gain on Forward-Exchange Contract		$40,000

to record the gain from the forward-exchange contract. The gain is equal to ($0.55 − $0.50) × FC 800,000.

3. At the date of the settlement, March 10, 19X4, there are three entries:
   a. To record the gain from the forward-exchange contract,

Foreign Currency Receivable from Exchange Broker	$80,000	
Deferred Gain on Forward-Exchange Contract		$80,000

where the gain equals ($0.65 − $0.55) × FC800,000.

   b. To record the payment of obligation to the exchange broker and the receipt of the foreign currency:

Payable to the Exchange Broker	$480,000	
Cash		$480,000
Foreign Currency	$520,000	
Foreign Currency Receivable from Exchange Broker		$520,000

   c. To record the cost of the merchandise received and the

payment of the foreign
currency to the supplier:

Deferred Gain on Forward-		
Exchange Contract	$120,000	
Equipment	$480,000	
Foreign Currency Premium		
on Forward-Exchange		
Contract		$80,000

Example 2: Hedge of an Exposed Net-Asset or Liability Position

On December 1, 19X3, to hedge an exposed liability position, the American National Company entered into a forward-exchange contract with an exchange broker for the delivery FC400,000 in 90 days. The following exchange rates are in effect on the following dates:

December 1, 19X3, Forward Rate: FC1 = $0.48
December 1, 19X3, Spot Rate: FC1 = $0.45
December 31, 19X3, Spot Rate: FC1 = $0.55
March 1, 19X4, Spot Rate: FC1 = $0.60

Because the contract qualifies as a hedge of an exposed liability position, the entries will be as follows:

1. At the date of the inception of the forward-exchange contract, December 10, 19X3,

Foreign Currency Receivable		
from Exchange Broker	$180,000	
Premium on Forward-		
Exchange Contract	$12,000	
Payable to Exchange		
Broker		$192,000

to record the receivable and payable relating to the forward contract.

2. At the balance sheet date, December 31, 19X3, the gain from the forward-exchange contract and the amortization of premium is recognized by the two entries that follow.

a. Foreign Currency Receivable-		
from Exchange Broker	$40,000	
Gain on Forward-		
Exchange Contract		$40,000

for a ($0.55 − $0.45) ×
FC400,000 gain.

b. Amortization of Premium on
   Forward-Exchange Contract $4,000
      Premium on Forward-
      Exchange Contract $4,000
   for a ($12,000/3) amortization
   amount.

3. At the date settlement, March 1, 19X4, there are three entries:
   a. To recognize the gain from the
      forward-exchange contract,
   Foreign Currency Receivable
   from Exchange Broker $20,000
      Gain on Forward-Exchange
      Contract $20,000
   where the gain equals ($0.60 −
   $0.55) × FC400,000.
   b. To record payment of the
      obligation to the exchange
      broker and the receipt of the
      foreign currency,
   Payable to Exchange Broker $192,000
      Cash $192,000
   Foreign Currency $240,000
      Foreign Currency
      Receivable
      from Exchange Broker $240,000
   c. To record the amortization of
   the premium,
   Amortization of Premium on
   Forward-Exchange Contract $8,000
      Premium on Forward-
      Exchange Contract $8,000

Example 3: Hedge of a Foreign Currency Speculation

On December 1, 19X3, to speculate in foreign currency market, the American National Company entered into a forward-exchange contract with an exchange broker for the delivery of FC400,000 in 60 days. Information about the exchange rates between the U.S. dollar and the foreign currency is as follows:

December 1, 19X3, 60-day Forward Rate: FC1 = $0.50

December 31, 19X3, 30-day Forward Rate: FC1 = $0.55
January 30, 19X4, Spot Rate: FC1 = $0.60

Because the contract qualifies as foreign currency speculation, the entries will be as follows:

1. At the date of the inception of the forward-exchange contract, December 1, 19X3,

Foreign Currency Receivable		
from Exchange Broker	$200,000	
Payable to Exchange		
Broker		$200,000

to record the receivable and payable relating to the forward contract.

2. At the balance sheet date, December 31, 19X3,

Foreign Currency Receivable		
from Exchange Broker	$20,000	
Gain on Forward-Exchange		
Contract		$20,000

to record the gain on the foreign exchange contract. The gain is computed as ($0.55 − $0.50) × FC400,000.

3. At the date of the settlement, January 30, 19X4, there are three entries:
   a. To recognize the gain from the forward-exchange contract,

Foreign Currency Receivable		
from Exchange Broker	$20,000	
Gain on Forward-Exchange		
Contract		$20,000

where the gain equals ($0.60 − $0.55) × FC400,000.

   b. To record the payment of the obligation to the exchange broker and the receipt of foreign currency,

Payable to Exchange Broker	$200,000	
Cash		$200,000
Foreign Currency	$240,000	
Foreign Currency		
Receivable from Exchange		
Broker		$240,000

c. To record the sale of foreign currency,

Cash	$240,000	
Foreign Currency		$240,000

ACCOUNTING FOR FUTURES CONTRACTS

Background

Multinational firms need to buy and sell various commodities that are traded on various exchanges around the world. These commodities include metals (gold, silver, platinum, copper, zinc, lead, etc.), meats (pork bellies, turkeys, cattle, etc.), grains (wheat, barley, oats, corn, etc.), unique items (eggs, soybeans, plywood and cotton), and financial instruments (bonds and notes, commercial paper, treasury bills, GNMA mortgages). Futures contracts are used by multinational firms to trade in these commodities. By definition, a futures contract is an exchange-traded contract between a futures exchange clearinghouse and a buyer and a seller for the future delivery of a standardized quantity of an item at a specified future date and at a specified price.

Statement of Financial Accounting Standards No. 80, Accounting for Futures Contracts, issued in August 1984, specifies the accounting treatment for exchange-traded futures contracts.

All forward contracts with an exchange broker have the following common characteristics:

1. The need for an initial margin deposit, paid to the broker, that represents a small portion of the futures contracts.
2. The need to readjust the deposit as the market value of the futures contract changes.
3. The need to close out the account by either receiving or delivering the item, paying out receiving cash, or entering into an offsetting contract.

A depiction of these characteristics follows:

When an enterprise enters into a futures contract with an exchange broker, an initial margin deposit is paid to the broker. The margin deposit usually represents a small fraction of the value of the futures contract. The deposit is recorded as an asset on the enterprise's books, but the value of the futures contract is recorded. As the market value of the futures contract changes, the change is reflected in the enterprise's account with the broker on a regular basis. When market changes increase the broker account, the enterprise may be able to withdraw cash from the account, and when market changes decrease the amount, the company may be required to pay additional cash to the broker to maintain a specified minimum balance in the broker's account. The futures contract may be closed out (canceled or settled) by either delivering or receiving, paying or receiving cash, or by entering into an offsetting contract. When the futures contract is closed out, the margin deposit is returned to the enterprise with the cash from the gains on the futures contract. If the enterprise suffers a loss on the futures contract, the margin deposit is offset against amounts to be paid by the enterprise to the broker.[1]

Accounting for futures contracts differs depending on whether or not the contract is accounted for as a hedge and, if it is a hedge, whether the hedged item is carried at market value, whether it is a hedge of an existing asset or liability position or a firm commitment, or if the contract is a hedge of an anticipated transaction.

Futures Contracts Not Accounted for as a Hedge

If the transaction does not qualify as a hedge because it does not relate to a hedged item (such as an asset or liability position, or firm commitment or an anticipated transaction), it is accounted for as a speculation in futures contracts. In the case of a futures contract not accounted for as a hedge, (1) the provisions of the Accounting Principles Board (APB) Opinion No. 30 are followed, and the gain or loss on the contract that is equal to the change in contract market price times the contract size is charged to income periods of change in value of the contract, and (2) the payables to a futures broker are classified as a current asset until the closing of the contract.

Example 1: Accounting for Futures Contracts Not Accounted for as Hedges

On October 1, 19X1, the Monti Futures Company purchases 100 February 1, 19X2, soybean futures contracts. The quoted market prices at the date of purchases is $5.80 a bushel; each contract covers 5,000 bushels. The initial margin deposit is $240,000. At the end of Year 1, the quoted market price of the soybean contract is $5.60 a bushel. The contract is closed on February 1, 19X2, when the quoted market price is $5.30 a bushel.

1. At the inception of the contract on October 1, 19X1,

| Deposit with Futures Broker | $240,000 | |
| Cash | | $240,000 |

to record the initial margin deposit when the contract is executed.

2. At the end of Year 1.

| Loss of Futures Contracts | $100,000 | |
| Payable to Futures Broker | | $100,000 |

to recognize losses on futures contracts of $0.20 per bushel ($5.80 − $5.60) on 500,000 bushel (500 × 100).

3. At the expiration of the contract on February 1, 19X2,

Payables to Futures Broker	$100,000	
Loss on Futures Contract	$150,000	
Cash		$250,000

to record the total loss on the contract, which is equal to ($5.60 − $5.30) × 500,000) and the $100,000 payment to the broker,

| Cash | $240,000 | |
| Deposit with Futures Broker | | $240,000 |

to record the return of the margin deposit by the broker.

Hedge Criteria

The accounting for futures contracts that qualify as hedges is different from the accounting for futures contracts that do not qualify as hedges. To qualify as a hedge according to SFAS 80, the contract must meet the following criteria:

1. The contract must be related to and designated as a hedge of identifiable assets, liabilities, firm commitments or anticipated transactions.
2. The hedged item must expose the firm to the risks of exchanges in price or interest rates. The determination of price risk is to be done on a decentralized basis when the firm is unable to do so at the firm level.
3. The changes in the market value of a futures contract must be highly correlated during the life of the contract with changes in a fair value of the

hedged item. The correlation must last if changes in the market value for the futures contract essentially offset changes in the fair value for the hedged item of the hedged item's interest expense or interest income.

After qualifying as a hedge by meeting these criteria, the accounting for futures contracts for each type of hedge item depends on whether the hedge item is reported at market value, whether it is a hedge of an existing asset or liability position or firm commitment, and whether it is a hedge of an anticipated transaction.

Example 2: Futures Contracts Accounted for as a Hedged Item Is Carried at Market Value

In such a case, both the changes in the values of the hedged asset and the related futures contract must be recognized in the same accounting period.

The unrealized change in the fair value of the item can be accounted for under one of two options: either (1) charge it to net income or (2) maintain it in a separate stockholders' equity account until sale or disposition of the hedged item.

The treatment of the changes in the market value of the related futures contract follows the option chosen for the changes in the fair market value of the hedged item. If the latter is charged to income, the changes in the market value of the related futures contract is also charged to income in which the market value changes. If the changes in the fair market value are charged to stockholders' equity account, the changes in the market value of the futures contract are also maintained in a stockholders' equity account until disposition of the related item.

The following example illustrates the accounting for futures contracts accounted for as a hedge when the hedged item is carried at market value: On November 1, 19XA, Precious Resources, Inc. has a gold inventory of 30,000 troy ounces, carried at a market value of $500 per ounce. The company expects to sell the gold in February 19XB, and sells 300 futures contracts of 100 troy ounces of gold each at a price for $500 per ounce to be delivered at the time of sale. A $250,000 deposit is required by the broker. At the end of year A, the market price is $530. In February of 19XB, the company sells the entire gold inventory at $550 per ounce and closes out the futures contract at the same price. The entries for the futures contract transactions are as follows:

1. At the inception of the contract on November 1, 19XA

| Deposit with the Futures Broker | $250,000 | |
| Cash | | $250,000 |

to make record of the initial margin deposit when the contract is executed.

2. At the end of Year A,

a. Gold Inventory	$900,000	
Unrealized Gain on Market		
Increase of Gold		$900,000

to recognize the changes in the fair market value of the gold inventory which equals ($530 − $500) × (30,000 troy ounces) = $900,000.

| b. Loss on Futures Contracts | $900,000 | |
| Payable to Futures Brokers | | $900,000 |

to recognize the loss on futures contracts which equals ($530 − $500) × (30,000 troy ounces) = $900,000.

3. At the expiration of the contract in February 19XB,

Cash	$16,500,000	
Gold Inventory		$15,900,000
Gains on Market Increase		
in Gold		$600,000

to recognize the sale of gold at $550 and the realization of a gain in the market increase in gold of $600,000 which is computed as ($550 − $530) × (30,000 troy ounces). The loss on futures contracts from December 1 through February is the $600,000 computed as above:

Payable to Futures Broker	$900,000	
Loss on Futures Contracts	$600,000	
Cash		$1,250,000
Deposit with Futures		
Broker		$250,000

Example 3: Futures Contracts Accounted for as a Hedge of an Existing Asset or Liability Position or a Firm Commitment

In such a case, any change in the market value of the futures contract is accounted for as an adjustment of the carrying value of the hedged item. If the contract is a hedge of a firm commitment, changes in the market value of the contract are included in the measurement of the transaction satisfying the commitment. If there is a difference between the contract price value of the hedged item and two conditions are met, the difference between the contract and the fair value of the hedged item is accounted for as a discount or a premium to be amortized as income over the life of the contract. The two conditions that need to be met are that (1) the hedged item is deliverable under contract and (2) the futures contract and the hedged item will be kept by the firm until the date of the delivery of the futures contract. If the two conditions are not met, then the difference between the contract price and the value of the hedged item is accounted for in the same manner as changes in contract value.

The following example illustrates accounting for futures contracts accounted for as hedge of an existing asset or liability position: On November 1, 19XA, Kalliopi Love Inc. has a soybean inventory of 30,000 bushels carried at a cost of $6.00 a bushel. The firms intend to sell the whole inventory by February 19XB. The firms sells six February 19XB futures contracts in November 19XA at a price of $6.50 per bushel. A $15,000 deposit is required by the broker. At the end of year A, the market price of soybeans is $7.10 per bushel. In February 19XB, the company sells the whole inventory at $6.30 per bushel and closes out the six futures contracts at the same price. The entries for the futures contracts transactions are as follows:

1. At the inception of the contract on November 1, 19XA,

Deposit with Futures Broker	$15,000	
Cash		$15,000

to make a record of the initial margin deposit when the contract is executed.

2. At the end of year A,

Deferred loss on Futures Contracts	$18,000	
Payable to Futures Broker		$18,000

to recognize the change in the market value of the contracts, which is calculated as ($7.10 − $6.50) × 30,000 = $18,000, and carry the deferred loss on futures contracts as a current asset.

3. At the expiration of the contract in February 19XB.

Cash	$21,000	
Payable to Futures Broker	$18,000	
Deferred Gain on Futures Contract		$24,000
Deposit with Futures Broker		$15,000

to recognize, at the expiration of the contract, (1) the deferred gain on futures contract, which is equal to ($7.10 − $6.30) × 30,000, and (2) the cash received from the broker ($15,000 deposit − $18,000 deferred loss to the broker + $24,000 gain on futures contract).

Deferred Gain on Futures Contracts	$24,000	
Deferred Loss on Futures Contracts		$18,000
Inventory		$6,000

to make an adjustment in carrying value of the hedged item.

Cash	$189,000	
Cost of Sales	$174,000	
Sales		$189,000
Inventory		$174,000

to recognize the sale of inventory (30,000 × $6.30) and the expending of the cost of inventory ($180,000 − $6,000).

Example 4: Futures Contracts Accounted for as a Hedge of an Anticipated Transaction

As stated above, when a futures contract is accounted for as a hedge, the hedge may be for an anticipated transaction that the firm intends or expects to enter into, but is not legally required to do so. Therefore, in such a situation, the futures contract does not relate to a firm's existing assets, liabilities or commitments. To qualify as a hedge of an anticipated transaction the following criteria need to be met: the terms and characteristics of the transactions are identifiable and the anticipated transaction is possible. If the two conditions are not met, the gain or loss on the contract is charged to income in the period of change in the market value of the contract. If the two conditions are met, the hedge qualifies as a hedge of an anticipated transaction and the following situations are possible:

1. If it is probable that the quantity of the anticipated transaction is less than the hedge, then the gains and losses on the contract in excess of the anticipated transaction are charged to income.
2. If the hedge is closed prior to the completion of the transaction, the changes in value are accumulated, carried forward and included in the anticipated transaction.
3. If the hedge is not closed prior to the completion of the transaction, the change in market value of the contract is accounted for in the same manner as the anticipated transaction.

The following example illustrates the accounting for a futures contract accounted for as a hedge of an anticipated transaction: The Champ Manufacturing Company uses gold in its finishing process. In October 19X1, it decides to acquire a contract of 30,000 ounces of gold at $500 per ounce. A $100,000 deposit is required by the broker. On February 1, 19X2, the Champ Manufacturing Company acquires 30,000 troy ounces for $520 per ounce and closes out the futures contract. The end of the fiscal year for the company is March 30. The entries for the futures contract transaction are as follows:

1. At the inception of the contract on October 1, 19X1,

Deposit with Futures Broker	$100,000	
Cash		$100,000

2. At the expiration of the contract on February 1, 19X2,

a. Cash	$700,000	
Deposit with Futures Broker		$100,000
Deferred Gain on Futures		
Contract		$600,000

to recognize the deferred gain on the futures contract, which is equal to ($520 − $500) × (30,000), and the cash received from the broker ($100,000 + $600,000).

b. Deferred Gain on Futures		
Contract	$600,000	
Raw Material Inventory (gold)	$15,000,000	
Cash		$15,600,000

to recognize the purchase of gold.

NOTE

1. Bill Jarnagin, *Financial Accounting Standards: Explanation and Analysis* (Chicago: Commerce Clearing House, 1988), pp. 977–78.

SELECTED READINGS

Kieso, Donald E., and Jerry J. Weygandt. *Intermediate Accounting*, 4th ed. New York: John Wiley & Sons, 1995.
Nikolai, Loren A., and John D. Bazely. *Intermediate Accounting*, 6th ed. Cincinnati, Ohio: South-Western Publishing Co., 1994.
Riahi-Belkaoui, Ahmed. *Accounting Theory*. London: Academic Press, 1992.
White, Gerald I., A. C. Sondhi, and Dov Fried. *The Analysis and Use of Financial Statements*. New York: John Wiley & Sons, 1994.

Index

About the Author

AHMED RIAHI-BELKAOUI is CBA Distinguished Professor of Accounting in the College of Business Administration, University of Illinois at Chicago. Author of more than 30 Quorum books and coauthor of several more, he is also a prolific author of articles published in the major scholarly and professional journals of his field, and has served on numerous editorial boards that oversee them.

ISBN 1-56720-116-4

EAN

9 781567 201161

HARDCOVER BAR CODE